Sacred

Balance

*How Ancient Practices
Can Restore Modern Minds*

MIRIAM DIEPHOUSE-McMILLAN

chalice
PRESS

Print: 9780827235670
EPUB: 9780827235687
EPDF: 9780827235694

ChalicePress.com

Contents

Introduction

Come to me, all you that are weary and are carrying heavy burdens, and I will give you rest. —Matthew 11:28

Our culture is facing a mental health crisis. One in five adults experiences some form of mental illness in any given year, and suicide has become the second leading cause of death among children aged ten to fourteen.[1] The isolation and anxiety of the COVID-19 pandemic only heightened the need for mental health awareness. Something is off-kilter in our society, and we need resources to help us restore the balance.

The number of people identifying as spiritual "seekers" is also increasing in contrast to those affiliating with organized religions. People are less interested in being told what to believe and more interested in how to engage in their own search for meaning. There's a longing for deeper spirituality alongside the search for mental well-being.

In writing *Sacred Balance*, I hope to speak to these needs. My work as a psychiatric hospital chaplain gives me daily opportunities to reflect on the search for mental and spiritual wholeness. Each person I meet, regardless of faith or cultural background, longs for the same basic things: joy, purpose, and connection. These goals are not new. Faith traditions have centuries of wisdom for directing our lives toward these spiritual values. In particular, I find that spiritual practices provide a helpful structure for our work toward healing and growth. I've also noticed that mental health research is starting to catch on to the wisdom of spiritual traditions. Many deeply rooted spiritual practices have proven benefits for our minds, bodies, and souls.

The relationship between mental health and religion has not always been a friendly one. As the fields of psychology and psychiatry

[1] "Mental Health By the Numbers," National Alliance on Mental Illness, accessed July 31, 2024, www.nami.org/about-mental-illness/mental-health-by-the-numbers.

developed in the mid-nineteenth century, they sought to establish themselves as scientific disciplines. Their founders were often skeptical or downright disdainful of religious beliefs. Freud famously dismissed religion as an illusion that humankind was ready to outgrow.[2] Some spiritual traditions responded to this derision by mistrusting the sciences all together. Religious leaders advised people to look to faith alone as a solution for their psychological troubles. Some, at times, viewed mental illness as a moral failing that required spiritual correction.[3] This increased the stigma of those who were suffering and caused deep spiritual distress by convincing people that a lack of faith caused their symptoms.

Although both sides have made progress, mutual distrust between psychiatry and spirituality still lingers today. I know professionals who dismiss patients' spirituality as a symptom of their illness. I also know patients who refuse treatment because they've been taught that their illness is a punishment from God. Overcoming this dangerous divide requires an active search for common ground.

Despite such a fraught history, faith and the mental health field share essential goals. The very names of their disciplines acknowledge a common foundation: psychology/psychiatry come from the Greek root *psyche*, meaning mind or soul; while spirituality comes from the Latin *spiritus*, meaning soul or spirit. There is clearly overlap between these terms. Both signify the unique core of a person—the part of us that transcends physicality and distinguishes us as individuals. Psychiatry and psychology approach this mind/soul/spirit from a research-based scientific perspective, while spirituality has an experiential and existential approach. Both sides recognize the potential for brokenness in our souls, and both aim to bring healing and restoration.

I am by no means implying that religion and psychiatric care are equivalent. This book is not intended as medical advice, and even the strongest faith is no substitute for medication and therapy. Rather, in highlighting the shared interest between the two, I hope to shift the perspective from competition to collaboration. Spirituality has a lot to offer people struggling with mental illness, and for their part faith communities could also learn plenty from the latest research on well-

---

[2] Kendra Cherry, "Sigmund Freud on Religion," *Verywell Mind*, November 6, 2023, www.verywellmind.com/freud-religion-2795858.

[3] For an in-depth history, see Heather Vacek, *Madness: American Protestant Responses to Mental Illness* (Waco, TX: Baylor University Press, 2015).

being. As I will show in the chapters that follow, there's increasing evidence that spiritual practices are beneficial for maintaining mental health.

Self-help culture is full of spiritual terms like "meditation," "gratitude," and "purpose." There seems to be growing awareness that spiritual traditions have something helpful to offer. Researchers can now study the physiological effects of prayer and other religious practices to understand more precisely how they affect our minds and bodies. In addition to these measurable benefits, spiritual practices provide existential value. We are meaning-making creatures. Spirituality is the avenue by which we explore our sense of purpose and connection to something beyond ourselves. A holistic understanding of mental well-being necessarily includes engagement with our core beliefs and practices. Faith traditions were around for thousands of years before what we now call mental health, and those faith traditions carry within them generations of wisdom about how we can tend to our souls.

Research on spirituality provides insight into how our beliefs and practices may help (or hinder) our psychological well-being. Studies on religious coping and mental illness, for example, highlight a distinction between religious belief and spiritual engagement. These studies suggest that the specific content of a person's belief, or even their attendance at religious services, is less significant than *how* they engage their faith.[4] In short, religion is a resource only to the degree that we actively use it to navigate the struggles and joys in our lives. This speaks to me of the importance of spiritual practices—tools that allow us to actively experience spiritual connection and pursue questions of meaning and purpose. I have chosen the spiritual practices in this book with this goal in mind. Each one is rooted in the teachings of Christian faith while also promoting attitudes and behaviors proven to support mental health.

My own spiritual heritage is Christian, so I write primarily from that point of view. I also recognize that spiritual traditions have been learning and borrowing from one another since the beginning of human history. Those familiar with mindfulness or Zen Buddhist traditions may recognize some values I've incorporated into my faith

---

[4] Kenneth Pargament and Curtis Brant, "Religion and Coping" in *Handbook of Religion and Mental Health*, ed. Harold Koenig (Academic Press, 1998), 111–28.

and practice. My work in an interfaith chaplaincy setting has given me great respect for the unique wisdom each tradition brings to the table. I've also noticed that the contemplative and mystical branches of many religions share common themes. There is significant overlap between the wisdom of reflective spirituality and the trends in modern mental health advice. The practices I offer in *Sacred Balance* are variations on these recurrent themes.

The first theme woven throughout the book is *intentionality.* Spiritual development and mental health maintenance both take commitment, not merely going through the motions. Attending to the needs of our souls requires our conscious choices. Our lives are busy, so it may take creativity to find the time and space we need to do this meaningful work. Consider setting aside a regular time for spiritual practice and identify a space where you are unlikely to be interrupted. You can adapt any of the practices I describe to the needs of your life, but be clear and thoughtful about how you do so. There is wisdom in the ancient tradition of designating times and places as sacred.

A second theme in the ancient wisdom of these practices is *connection.* By definition, spirituality links us to something larger than ourselves. We are not made to live in isolation, so we need this connection to maintain well-being. The practices I include in this book connect us consciously to God, to ourselves, and to the world around us. They can help us experience God's presence in a more holistic, embodied way. Through such practices we can shift from cognitive beliefs about God's love to a real experiential understanding of ourselves as beloved children. As this knowledge takes root in our souls, it becomes a source of great strength and courage. Tapping into God's infinite compassion transforms our attitude toward others and motivates us to action. Spiritual connection leads us toward the work of love and justice in the world.

A final theme across these practices is *self-compassion.* Spiritual practices can help us build an attitude of acceptance toward ourselves and our daily experiences. Connecting with God enables us to see ourselves without the filter of criticism we often habitually apply. We gradually learn to let go of our expectations and accept our experiences just as they are. This requires acknowledging our limitations and not setting unrealistic goals for our practice. We are finite human beings with limited energy and resources. The practices in this book will not change that. We may not have a profound spiritual awakening, and that is OK. We are still engaging our faith in a powerful way by choosing to connect with God in whatever state we find ourselves right now and letting that be enough. Spirituality is more of a journey and relationship than an achievement. We can find wisdom and healing by showing compassion to ourselves along the way.

Sacred Balance is essentially a toolbox. In it, I've identified nine practices that have served me well in my personal and professional spiritual work. Each practice offers unique benefits for deepening faith and enhancing mental health. Yet this collection of tools is neither exhaustive nor prescriptive. You may find that some are especially useful to you while others don't quite fit your needs. You may already have tools that help you, and these nine practices can supplement what you are already doing. Each chapter introduces a particular spiritual practice. I set the stage, give an overview of the practice, and provide some history on how the practice developed from Christian scripture and tradition. I highlight the potential mental health benefits of the practice then offer step-by-step instructions for how to try it out yourself. There are tips for getting started and adapting the practice to your own lifestyle, as well as reflection questions to help you consider how the practice is working for you. This structure is intended as a guide you can use as it best serves you. If history is not your thing, feel free to skip that section. If you're already convinced that a practice is good to try, go ahead and jump right to the instructions. All of the practices inform one another, but there is no particular order in which they have to be done. Start with the chapters that catch your eye or relate to a particular issue you're encountering. The Appendix: Ways to Use this Book (beginning on page 89) offers detailed suggestions for engaging the practices I've outlined, either independently or with a group. Focus on what works for you.

*****

Wherever you find yourself on the journey toward mental and spiritual well-being, I'm glad you're here. I invite you to take a moment to reflect on what prompted you to pick up this book.

- What questions are you pondering? *how to move past fears,*

- What are your goals for mental health and spiritual development? *peace, quiet, acceptance of others and self*

- What barriers may get in the way?   *me*

- What hopes, fears, and longings do you carry with you?   *closeness with grandkids, Fear of time passing and my complacency*

   Reflect prayerfully on these questions as you dive into the practices and find your own sacred balance.

CHAPTER 1

Contemplation: Centering Prayer

Be still, and know that I am God. —Psalm 46:10

Stillness is a foreign concept to many of us. The cultural pressures to stay busy and productive keep us rushing through our days without much time to stop and think. On the rare occasions we get a chance to sit down and rest, we tend to fill that time with entertainment and social media. Sitting in stillness without an activity or concrete goal is so unfamiliar to us that it can be unsettling when we first try it. Letting go of all the busyness feels like wasting time or missing opportunities. It brings up doubts about our ability to keep up with what the world demands of us. It can be scary, and often this fear leads us to jump back into action just to escape our own thoughts.

And yet God calls us to be still. God invites us to know and rest in God's presence. When the world insists that we keep busy and prove our worth by accomplishing tasks, God calls us to stop *doing* and just *be*. At the heart of this call to stillness is a gentle reminder that our value lies not in our to-do list but in our identity as God's beloved children. God encourages stillness so we can stop and remember that central truth. Over the centuries, Christians responding to this invitation have described a state of *contemplation*, or deep reflection, that goes beyond words to fully experience God's loving presence. Such contemplation is an antidote to the toxic stress and anxiety generated by our productivity culture.

Centering Prayer provides a framework for sitting in stillness with God. It helps us open ourselves to the experience of contemplation so we can rest in God's healing love. Stillness and rest are always therapeutic. As I will highlight later in this chapter, research increasingly supports the benefits of various types of meditation practices. Centering Prayer shares these proven effects while grounding us in the truth that God is the source of our rejuvenation. Rooted solidly in centuries of Christian contemplative practices, Centering Prayer is a powerful tool for releasing the grip of our modern anxieties.

What is Centering Prayer?

Centering Prayer is different from the traditional style of prayer with which many of us are familiar. We're often taught that prayer is a conversation—expressing ourselves, making requests, or reciting certain words. By contrast, in Centering Prayer, we *experience* God's presence rather than talking to God. It's like a young child resting in a trusted parent's lap for comfort and connection. When my two-year-old daughter curls up next to me on the couch, she doesn't need to ask for anything. My presence is enough to remind her she is safe and loved. To experience God in this way we must slow down, quiet our minds, and be receptive to God's presence within us and around us.

In contrast to the constant noise of our busy lives (and even our own thoughts), Centering Prayer requires space for silence. Thomas Merton, a twentieth-century American monk, described it as "making use of no words and no thoughts at all."[1] If this description of sitting in silence and trying to clear your thoughts sounds suspiciously like meditation to you, your instincts are correct. There are other similar techniques, each rooted in their own religious and cultural traditions. While Centering Prayer has much in common with these other meditation practices, it's uniquely grounded in the relational nature of Christian faith. The goal of Centering Prayer is not absence or emptiness but true Presence. We sit in stillness and quiet our minds to make space for the One who is already there. Such unstructured silence doesn't come naturally to most of us, but it gets easier with time and practice. Centering Prayer is a tool for increasing our capacity to rest in God's loving embrace.

The practice of Centering Prayer requires both attention and intention. We choose to focus our awareness on God's presence instead of the contents of our own thoughts. This may require letting go of our expectations about what God is like or how prayer should

---

[1] Thomas Merton, *Contemplative Prayer* (New York: Doubleday, 1969), 19.

feel. Centering Prayer is not a means to some other end; being with God is the end itself. We can let go of trying to make things happen and instead create space for deeper awareness of God's presence. This awareness is itself a gift from God. It's not something we achieve by "doing it right." God is already embracing us in love, and all we need is to open ourselves to it.

The organization Contemplative Outreach offers this succinct description of Centering Prayer as "prayer in which we experience God's presence within us, closer than breathing, closer than thinking, closer than consciousness itself."[2] This experience of God's presence is so contrary to our cultural expectations of productivity that it can be hard to wrap our minds around it. It transcends our ability to fully understand or describe it. Thankfully, we have the wisdom and witness of Christians across thousands of years to help us. Many of them answered God's invitation to stillness and passed down their experiences in the form of contemplative prayer traditions.

Centering Prayer in Scripture and Tradition

The roots of contemplative prayer trace back to the early centuries of Christianity. Writings from a group of ascetic hermits in northern Africa known as the Desert Elders (or Desert Fathers, though several were women) emphasize meditating on scripture and praying "from the heart" rather than with words.[3] They describe the value of silence and the need to create space for the awareness of God's mystery.[4] These writings shaped the foundations of Christian monastic traditions in both Eastern and Western branches of the church. Monastic communities in turn preserved and adapted specific prayer practices to encourage spiritual contemplation.

In Eastern Orthodox Christianity, a tradition known as *hesychasm* grew out of the contemplative teachings of the Desert Elders. The name *hesychasm* itself derives from the Greek word for stillness. *Hesychasts* developed a practice known as "the Jesus Prayer," which entails meditative repetition of the words "Lord Jesus Christ, Son of God, have mercy on me, a sinner." By invoking the name of Jesus continuously throughout daily tasks, the *hesychasts* sought to move

---

[2] "Centering Prayer," Contemplative Outreach, accessed August 11, 2023, https://www.contemplativeoutreach.org/centering-prayer-method/.

[3] Merton, *Contemplative Prayer*, xxix.

[4] Merton, *Contemplative Prayer*, 19.

beyond words to a "prayer of the whole person—no longer something that we think or say, but something that we are."[5]

The legacy of contemplative prayer in Western Christianity is most evident in the Catholic monastic traditions. Figures such as Saint Augustine and Saint Gregory the Great up through medieval mystics like Bernard of Clairvaux, Hildegard of Bingen, Meister Eckhart, and Julian of Norwich all cultivated spiritual practices that sought to foster experiential knowledge of God's love.[6] Their writings highlight the relational nature of contemplation, often using romantic or erotic imagery to describe the heart's ultimate desire for resting in God's presence. Modern writers like Thomas Merton and Evelyn Underhill carried these strands of contemplative spirituality into the twentieth century.

Alongside these well-established branches of Christian tradition, less privileged communities developed their own expressions of contemplative prayer. Barbara Holmes, for example, traces the vibrant history of contemplative practices in the black church.[7] She notes how activists like Martin Luther King Jr. and Nelson Mandela drew on the spiritual practices of stillness in promoting nonviolent resistance. Holmes argues that transcendent experiences of God's presence in oppressed communities often serve to ground and strengthen their movements of social justice.

From hermits and monastics to leaders and activists, Christians across thousands of years and nearly every continent have responded to the invitation to be still and know God's presence. Recent interest in rejuvenating contemplative prayer traditions stems from a recognition that this ancient wisdom has something crucial to offer the contemporary church. In the twentieth century a group of American Trappist monks whose work is continued by the organization Contemplative Outreach popularized Centering Prayer as a particular tool for contemplative practice.[8] Their legacy is only one of many

---

[5] Kallistos Ware, *The Orthodox Way* (Yonkers, NY: St. Vladimir's Seminary Press, 1995), 123.

[6] "The Christian Contemplative Tradition," Contemplative Outreach, accessed January 28, 2024, https://www.contemplativeoutreach.org/the-christian-contemplative-tradition/.

[7] Barbara Holmes, *Joy Unspeakable: Contemplative Practices of the Black Church* (Minneapolis, MN: Fortress, 2017).

[8] "History of Contemplative Outreach," Contemplative Outreach, accessed January 31, 2024, https://www.contemplativeoutreach.org/history-of-contemplative-outreach.

strands of contemplative Christian spirituality, but the format of Centering Prayer provides an accessible entry point for anyone interested in exploring contemplative practice.

Why Try Centering Prayer?

Centering Prayer is a holistic practice, meaning it can help integrate our mind, body, and spirit. This may be why contemplative practices have such a rich heritage throughout Christian history. We often compartmentalize our lives and focus on one piece at a time. But in calling us to stillness, God invites us to bring our whole selves. What we know and believe in our minds is important. But so is what we experience in our bodies and how we feel in our spirits. Centering Prayer connects our mind, body, and spirit together as we sit in God's presence. It also offers specific benefits on each of these levels:

Mind

Calming our minds and learning to observe thoughts without engaging them can reduce anxiety and increase our sense of peace. Anxiety tells us we must keep *doing* in order to be safe or valued. Centering Prayer is the exact opposite. The more time we spend resting in God's presence, the easier it is to combat all those pressures to do and achieve. Studies show that over time meditation practices can re-wire our brains to be less agitated, calmer, and more compassionate.[9]

God's call to "be still and know that I am God" is more than just an invitation to rest. It's also a reminder that we are not the ones in charge. The expectation that we can control and perfect everything about our lives is a false hope that sets us up for frustration. Centering Prayer can help us to acknowledge our limitations and reframe our concerns in light of God's bigger picture. It's like checking a compass to help orient our minds to the true north of God's presence. Resting in that presence allows us to accept life as it is and maintain hope beyond our own limited resources.

---

[9] See the research of Sara Lazar, Ph.D. ("Lazar Lab for Meditation Research," Massachusetts General Hospital, accessed December 12, 2023, https://www.massgeneral.org/psychiatry/research/lazar-lab-for-meditation-research) and Andrew Newberg, M.D. ("Research," Marcus Institute of Integrated Health, Thomas Jefferson University Hospital, accessed December 12, 2023, http://www.andrewnewberg.com/research/).

Body

Regularly practicing Centering Prayer can help our bodies transition from the stress mode of daily life into a state of healing and restoration. When we never stop moving, thinking, and planning, our bodies maintain a constant level of fight-or-flight adrenaline. We don't get a chance to heal. God did not create us to run nonstop, and the Bible is full of reminders to rest![10] Centering Prayer makes intentional time for the stillness our bodies need.

Popular health and wellness culture is full of research about the physical benefits of meditation practices. Websites and magazines highlight improvements in everything from sleep and digestion to blood pressure and pain management.[11] Centering Prayer anchors this healing power in the Creator who knit our bodies together. Spending time in God's presence helps us experience our bodies in an awe-inspired and compassionate way, remembering we are "fearfully and wonderfully made."[12]

Spirit

Centering Prayer differs from other forms of meditation in helping us cultivate awareness of God's presence. We are not merely sitting still: we are sitting *with God*. Like any relationship, our connection with God grows the more quality time we put into it. Centering Prayer is "both a relationship with God and a discipline to deepen that relationship."[13] We are prioritizing quality time with God.

Our time in God's presence provides the foundation for how we live out our faith day to day. Spending time with God helps us to realign our values and priorities. It deepens our commitment to advance God's work in the world. As Barbara Holmes describes it, contemplative practice "awakens a palpable and actionable love ... a

---

[10] See, for example, Exodus 20:8–11, Exodus 33:14, Matthew 11:28, and Hebrews 4:9–11.

[11] See, for example, "Meditation: A Simple, Fast Way to Reduce Stress," Mayo Clinic, last updated December 14, 2023, https://www.mayoclinic.org/tests-procedures/meditation/in-depth/meditation/art-20045858, and Cynthia Allen, "The Potential Health Benefits of Meditation," *American College of Sports Medicine's Health & Fitness Journal* 24, no. 6 (November 2020): 28–32, https://doi.org/10.1249/FIT.0000000000000624.

[12] Psalm 139:14.

[13] Contemplative Outreach, "Centering Prayer."

'fire shut up in the bones' that inspires action."[14] When our minds and bodies can rest in God's presence, we are nourished and strengthened for God's work of restoration.

Calming our minds, resting our bodies, and deepening our faith all grow out of the seemingly simple practice of sitting in stillness with God. Centering Prayer "has the potential to heal, instruct, and connect us to the source of our being."[15] These benefits develop gradually with time and practice. Centering Prayer is not a magic solution to stress, but it offers a much-needed counterbalance to the pressures the world imposes on us.

How to Practice Centering Prayer

Centering Prayer is a simple practice, but that doesn't mean it's easy! My first time practicing it felt like the longest ten minutes of my life. My mind was in overdrive, jumping from one thought to the next. I was so focused on doing the practice "right" that I spent most of the prayer time anxiously criticizing my own thoughts. It takes a lot of practice to find and experience stillness. Sometimes the stillness can feel really uncomfortable, or it may allow difficult emotions to surface.[16] This doesn't mean you're doing it wrong. Try to let go of specific goals or expectations for this time with God. Offer compassion to yourself for whatever arises, remembering that God is present with you.

1) Set your intention.

Make plans to spend this time with God, just as you might make a coffee date with a friend. Rather than trying to pray hurriedly between tasks, or while dozing off at the end of the day, establish a deliberate plan for when and where you will pray. Set a timer for how long you want to spend in prayer so you don't have to look at a clock or worry about when to be done. (See below for tips on how long to try it!) Sit in a quiet, comfortable place where you can relax and focus.

---

[14] Holmes, *Joy Unspeakable*, 17.

[15] Holmes, *Joy Unspeakable*, 5.

[16] My favorite yoga teacher is fond of talking about the difference between discomfort and pain. If this practice makes you feel unsafe or brings up truly painful experiences, please seek the help of a mental health practitioner. They can help you find safe and healthy ways to process your experience and offer guidance about if/when to try Centering Prayer again.

2) Choose a sacred word.

Select a word that represents your intention to be with God. Close your eyes and silently introduce your sacred word. The purpose of the sacred word is to clarify your intention and ground yourself when your thoughts inevitably wander. You can choose any word or phrase that helps you connect to God's presence, such as "grace," "stillness," or "God with us." Simplicity is key here; longer phrases can be more distracting than centering. A visual image such as a candle flame or a clear lake may also work as a focal point for your prayer. Some people prefer to always use the same word, while others find a new sacred word or phrase each time they pray.

3) Notice distractions—then come back.

Your thoughts will wander. Use your sacred word as an anchor to bring yourself back whenever this happens. Observe your thoughts and feelings without engaging them. For example, if you catch yourself worrying, gently say to yourself, "I'm worrying about X. I can come back to that later." Try not to get frustrated about the distractions; simply notice them and go back to your sacred word. Repeat this process until your timer goes off.

4) End in silence.

A few moments of silence at the end of your prayer can ease the transition back to whatever else may be on your plate. Instead of jumping abruptly to your next task, take time to reflect on your experience. Allow yourself to carry this awareness of God's presence into the rest of your day.

Tips for Practicing Centering Prayer

Start small. Don't try to sit down for a thirty-minute session your first time. Start with two to five minutes. Even this may feel very long at first. As you become used to the time of quiet focus, gradually increase the time you spend in each prayer session.

Make it a habit. The benefits of contemplative prayer develop over time. Try to practice at the same time every day. Build it into your routine, or put a reminder on your phone or planner so you don't forget.

Let go of expectations. There is no specific goal in Centering Prayer other than spending time with God. Don't get discouraged if you're not feeling focused or having a profound spiritual experience. You are present, and God is with you. That is the whole point. Try to keep your heart and mind open.

Reflection

Once you've had a chance to try Centering Prayer a few times, take a moment to reflect using the questions below. You can journal your responses, talk to a friend or spiritual director, or think through them silently.

- What was your experience of Centering Prayer like?
- What came up for you during or after the time of prayer?
- What do you find challenging about this style of prayer?
- What do you find helpful or appealing about it?
- What, if anything, got in the way of your intention to practice Centering Prayer?
- What would you like to continue or change about your practice going forward?

CHAPTER 2

Discernment: Daily Examen

Test everything; hold fast to what is good.
—1 Thessalonians 5:21

Have you ever stood in the grocery store and felt overwhelmed by the multitude of choices? To me it can seem as if every item on my grocery list comes in a dozen different flavors, brands, prices, and packaging. Do I get the cheapest one? What social and environmental impacts should I consider? Which product will my family like best? All these complex factors go into one simple decision. Multiply that by the number of choices we face in a given day or week, and it's a recipe for decision fatigue.

With so many options and opinions in every arena of life, it can be hard to keep track of our own priorities. On one hand it's a blessing to have such freedom to choose. We have the power to decide how we spend our time and where we put our resources. Each decision is an opportunity to express ourselves and our values. On the other hand, we can easily become overwhelmed by all the choices we have to make and why. Without a clear sense of purpose, we risk making choices that don't align with our beliefs.

Christian faith gives us some direction: we seek God's will as a guiding force behind our decisions, but it can be hard to know what that really means. Scripture points to God's overarching plans for peace on earth and human flourishing, but even that can seem abstract. So much of our modern life seems outside the scope of biblical guidance. Does God care what kind of cars we buy? Which movies we watch? What we eat for dinner? If so, how are we supposed to figure it out?

We are not the first to ask these questions. Faithful Christians for thousands of years have struggled to discern God's will and apply it to their lives. Thankfully, some of them passed along wisdom and tools to help us find more connections between our faith and our daily life. There are spiritual practices specifically designed to aid our process of discernment. The Daily Examen is one such tool that can help us reflect on the details of our lives with an eye toward how God is already working and where God might be calling us in the future.

What Is the Daily Examen?

The Daily Examen is a specific tool for practicing discernment. *Discernment* is one of those "churchy" sounding words often reserved for pastors and seminary students. It sometimes describes the process of exploring a call to ministry, but it also has a much broader meaning. *Discernment is the Christian practice of seeking the guidance of the Holy Spirit in our daily lives.* If we truly believe our actions matter to God, then it's worth taking time to reflect on those actions. *Discernment means observing our daily choices to see how we can better align our lives with what God is doing in the world.*

We commonly pray for God's guidance in difficult situations or before important life events, but the answers often take some work to interpret. Despite my most heartfelt prayers, I've never received direct verbal instructions from God telling me what to do. I've had to look for the answers that emerge from my daily experiences. Discernment is that intentional effort to follow up on our prayers for guidance. It's a form of active listening that allows us to sift out the voice of God from all the other noise in our lives.

The Daily Examen provides a structure for this discernment process. It's a practice of daily prayerful reflection on the events of our lives, with the goal of becoming more aware of God's spirit at work. Reviewing our experiences in conversation with God each day can help us notice things we would otherwise miss. When used over time, the Examen highlights patterns that can inform our future decisions.

Fr. Dennis Hamm, SJ, calls the Daily Examen "rummaging for God." He likens it to "going through a drawer full of stuff, feeling around, looking for something that you are sure must be in there somewhere."[1] We know and believe God is at work in our lives, but it can be hard to see how through all the other junk in the way. The Daily Examen gives us a chance to sort it all out.

As we sift through the events of each day, we can sort them into two helpful categories to help us notice where God is at work. The tradition of spiritual discernment calls these categories *consolation* and *desolation*, but they are essentially states of connection or disconnection from God. We can recognize them by the types of thoughts and feelings they evoke in us throughout the day.

Consolation is the experience of connectedness with God. It often prompts feelings of joy, peace, and gratitude. But this connectedness brings more than superficial happiness: it often feels spiritually energizing or deeply peaceful. In times of consolation you may notice a sense of purpose and motivation or the satisfaction that you are living out your beliefs and values. Consolation often enables you to feel more open and compassionate toward others.

Desolation, by contrast, is a feeling of disconnection from God. It's often accompanied by emotions of fear, sadness, anxiety, or guilt. Times of desolation can feel spiritually empty, hopeless, or meaningless. In such times, you might find yourself questioning your faith or losing interest in it all together. Desolation is often very self-focused and can lead us to withdraw from others or to become overly critical.

Everyone experiences times of consolation and desolation in their lives. The goal is not to get rid of desolation all together but to see what can be learned from both states. An attitude of nonjudgmental observation enables us to review the ups and downs of our day without setting up expectations of what we may find. Saint Ignatius called this attitude "indifference," but that doesn't mean we don't care.[2] Instead, being indifferent is an invitation to let go of control and be open to whatever insights arise from the Examen practice.

Recognizing patterns of consolation and desolation can give us information about where God is working. We start to notice which activities and experiences lead us to feel more connected to God and what parts of our lives contribute to disconnection. The Daily Examen

---

[1] Fr. Dennis Hamm, SJ, "Rummaging for God: Praying Backward through Your Day," *IgnatianSpirituality.com*, accessed March 17, 2024, https://www.ignatianspirituality.com/ignatian-prayer/the-examen/rummaging-for-god-praying-backward-through-your-day/.

[2] George E. Ganss, SJ, ed., *Ignatius of Loyola: The Spiritual Exercises and Selected Works* (Mahwah, NJ: Paulist Press, 1991), 392.

helps us to keep track of these patterns so that we can intentionally start choosing the things that nourish consolation. The more we do this, the easier it is to make daily choices and feel confident about where we direct our time and energy.

Daily Examen in Scripture and Tradition

Christian discernment has its roots in scripture. Paul lists "discernment of spirits" among the spiritual gifts in 1 Corinthians 12:8–11, and 1 John 4:1 advises believers to "test the spirits to see whether they are from God." To our modern ears, this language of "spirits" may call up images of supernatural beings, but that's not necessarily what it means. Christian tradition has long connected these "spirits" to our own inner impulses.[3] Discernment of spirits means testing whether our motivations and decisions align with God's purposes or not. Hebrews 5:14 suggests that this ability to distinguish good from evil is a mark of spiritual maturity that comes with practice.[4]

The earliest Christian writers highlighted discernment as a crucial element of spiritual growth. The Desert Elders encouraged reflection on one's thoughts to increase spiritual insight and prevent extremism.[5] They taught that thoughts have different sources: some are from God, some are from the devil, and some from ourselves.[6] The theme of discerning spirits also appears in the writings of Origen, Augustine, and Gregory the Great.[7]

In the sixteenth century Saint Ignatius of Loyola developed a concrete structure for spiritual discernment that we now know as the Daily Examen. While recovering from a battle wound, Ignatius had a conversion experience that inspired him to lead others toward greater union with Christ. He wrote *The Spiritual Exercises*, a kind of instruction manual for spiritual development. The *Exercises* outlines a thirty-day retreat program designed to be led by a spiritual director, but

---

[3] Kenneth Leech, *Soul Friend: Spiritual Direction in the Modern World* (Harrisburg, PA: Morehouse Publishing, 2001), 124.

[4] "But solid food is for the mature, for those whose faculties have been trained by practice to distinguish good from evil." (NRSVUE).

[5] Leech, *Soul Friend*, 38–39.

[6] John of Cassian, Conference I, Chapter 19, "Of the Three Origins of Our Thoughts," *Conferences of J. Cassian*, trans. Edgar C.S. Gibson, from A Select Library of Nicene and Post-Nicene Fathers of the Christian Church (New York: 1894), Christian Classics Ethereal Library, accessed March 17, 2024, https://ccel.org/ccel/cassian/conferences/conferences.ii.iii.xix.html.

[7] Leech, *Soul Friend*, 124.

its individual components can easily be applied to other contexts.[8] His framework for an "Examination of Conscience" forms the foundation of the modern practice of Daily Examen. He lays out the hallmarks of consolation and desolation, as well as guidelines for how to respond in one state versus the other.[9]

Since Ignatius, the practice of the Daily Examen has been well preserved through the legacy of spiritual direction. Spiritual direction is a form of mentoring and guidance focused on discerning God's will in the life of the directee. (Take a look at chapter 9 for more on this valuable practice.) Many spiritual directors use the Daily Examen to help directees explore questions of meaning and decision-making. The rich tradition of spiritual discernment represented in Ignatius' Daily Examen offers a valuable pathway for connecting faith and daily action.[10]

Why Try the Daily Examen?

Paying attention to the small ups and downs of each day can give us considerable insight into our overall well-being. This insight can help clarify our decisions and priorities and identify sources of stress as well as what brings us joy and peace. The more we recognize the roots of our consolation and of our desolation, the more freedom we find to choose what is life-giving.

The spiritual categories of consolation and desolation don't necessarily correspond to our overall mental health, but they can serve as guideposts directing us toward sources of support and healing. Our emotional life is not separate from our spirituality. In fact, the two often inform and enhance each other. Activities that bring us closer to God naturally bring a sense of peace and joy, while a pervasive pattern of desolation may serve as a warning sign that something is not right. Regular attention to these signs ensures we can reach out for help when we need it.[11]

---

[8] Keith R. Anderson and Randy D. Reese, *Spiritual Mentoring: A Guide for Seeking and Giving Direction* (Downers Grove, IL: InterVarsity Press, 1999).

[9] Ganss, *Ignatius*, 202.

[10] "Today the recovery of the tradition of spiritual discernment is in part the recovery of the unity of spirituality and moral and social action." Leech, *Soul Friend*, 125.

[11] If you notice any unusual patterns in your mood, please reach out to a qualified mental health professional. They can not only assess whether your experience is situational or may be symptomatic of a larger issue, but can also advise you on how to cope with whatever you're experiencing.

The Daily Examen shares some similarity with tools used in the mental health field for observing patterns in our emotional life. Often called mood trackers, these tools are available in a variety of formats for daily reflection on our thoughts and feelings.[12] Checking in with ourselves daily gives us a better picture of what's really going on. When we understand our habitual patterns, we handle stressful situations more effectively. Instead of falling into automatic habits, we can choose how we want to respond. We start to recognize problems early, before they get out of hand. The Daily Examen situates this self-reflection within the framework of faith, recognizing God as the grounding force that sustains our well-being. As we learn more about ourselves, we also learn to listen more deeply to the guidance of the Holy Spirit.

Daily reflection helps us to step back from the intensity of our thoughts and emotions and to observe them from another perspective. Regular practice of the Daily Examen can help us develop a neutral (or indifferent) stance toward our experiences. Jon Kabat-Zinn, proponent of Mindfulness-Based Stress Reduction, uses language from the Zen tradition to describe this insight. Terms like "non-judgment" and "non-striving" describe a similar attitude to what Ignatius called "indifference."[13] Both describe the ability to observe thoughts and emotions without being too attached to any specific outcome. A neutral stance helps us accept our thoughts and feelings as they are, without expecting anything different or criticizing what we observe. The spiritual perspective of the Examen adds a layer of trust to this neutrality. When we fully let go of our judgments and expectations, we can rest in the assurance that God is at work. The ultimate goal of our "indifference" is to set aside our limited outlook in exchange for the divine perspective on our lives.

Faithful discernment practice enhances our capacity to live with a clear sense of purpose. By relating our daily experiences to the ultimate question of God's calling in our lives, the Daily Examen can help us find meaning in our choices. Searching for meaning is crucial to human existence and survival.[14] Contemporary research on

---

[12] See, for example, "How to Use a Mood Tracker," *Verywell Mind*, accessed March 11, 2024. https://www.verywellmind.com/what-is-a-mood-tracker-5119337.

[13] Jon Kabat-Zinn, *Full Catastrophe Living: Using the Wisdom of Your Body and Mind to Face Stress, Pain, and Illness*, rev. ed., (New York: Bantam, 2013), 21–23, 26–27.

[14] Viktor Frankl, *Man's Search for Meaning*, rev. ed. (Washington Square Press, 1984), 121.

resilience highlights the value of meaning-making in recovery from trauma and adverse experiences.[15] As Christians, we find our ultimate meaning in our identity as children of God. Discernment is the work of connecting that identity to our daily experiences so our actions and choices reflect this central truth.

The Daily Examen always invites us to look forward. It helps us take what we've learned and use it to guide our future choices. The practice of spiritual discernment can help with making decisions, exploring vocational questions, and adjusting to changes in our lives. It can give purpose to the seemingly mundane choices we make every day. As we start to see where God is already at work, we can more easily follow the Spirit toward new ways to live out our faith.

How to Practice the Daily Examen

The Examen is most helpful when done regularly. Ideally this means committing to daily practice, but you can still benefit from taking the time to reflect every few days or even once a week. Ignatius' original instructions assume a thirty-day retreat, but you may need more or less time depending on your discernment goals. The key is to do it frequently enough that you can remember the basic events of your day/week and to keep it up long enough to observe patterns over time.

1) Become aware of God's presence.

Before you dive into reviewing your day, set your focus and intention. Invite God to join you as you look through the events of the day. Ask for clarity and wisdom. If there's a particular issue you'd like help discerning, lift it up to God before you begin.

2) Review the day with gratitude.

Walk through the day with God alongside you, as if you were narrating your activities to a friend. Notice even the smallest details. Use the following questions to guide your reflection:

---

[15] See, for example, Martin Seligman, "PERMA and the Building Blocks of Well-Being," *The Journal of Positive Psychology* 13, no. 4 (2018): 333–335, doi:10.1 080/17439760.2018.1437466; and Steven Southwick, et al., "Meaning, Purpose, and Growth" in *Resilience: The Science of Mastering Life's Greatest Challenges*, 3rd ed., (Cambridge, UK: Cambridge University Press: 2023), 193–208.

- *Which events, situations, or people do I feel particularly thankful for?*
- *When in my day did I feel most connected to God?*
- *When did I feel most distant from God?*

3) Pay attention to your emotions.

Notice any aspects of your day that brought up particular feelings. When did you feel happy? Sad? Angry? Afraid? Try to let go of any judgments about these emotions and simply observe when and how they arose. Consider what God might be saying to you through the various emotions you felt during the day.

4) Choose one feature of the day to pray about.

Identify an event or situation from your day about which you'd like help or wisdom. Take a few minutes to lift it up to God. Try to maintain a neutral perspective as you share your concerns, remembering the attitude of "indifference." Allow space for new insights to arise.

5) Look toward tomorrow.

Consider any new perspectives that emerged from your prayer. Where do you see God at work, and how might you participate in that work? Are there any changes you feel called to make? Ask for God's continuing guidance as you prepare for the coming day.

Tips for Practicing the Daily Examen

Use a journal. Record your reflections each time you pray the Examen. Look back on your journaling every few weeks and note any patterns in your observations.

Set a regular time. Practice the Examen just before you get ready for bed or first thing in the morning to look back at the previous day. You could also use your daily commute or another routine activity when your mind is free to reflect.

Respond with wisdom. Use your observations to help guide your actions going forward. Below are some guidelines on how to respond when we find ourselves in states of consolation and desolation.[16]

---

[16] Adapted from "Discernment: Consolation and Desolation," Loyola Press, accessed March 26, 2024, https://www.loyolapress.com/our-catholic-faith/ignatian-spirituality/discernment/discernment-consolation-and-desolation.

In times of desolation:

Ask God for help.

Seek out companionship.

Don't make or change any major decisions.

Remember a time of consolation and reflect on it.

In times of consolation:

Express gratitude to God.

Savor the moment, and fix it in your memory. Return to it when things get hard.

Use your energy to work toward your goals and commitments.

Reflection

After praying the Examen for a few weeks, use the following questions to reflect on your experience of practicing discernment. You can journal your responses, talk to a friend or spiritual director, or think through them silently. Notice any patterns or themes that have emerged from your daily prayer time.

- What was it like to review each day prayerfully?
- Where did you find the most consolation?
- What were sources of desolation for you?
- If you have you noticed any patterns about how God shows up in your life, what are they?
- What are you feeling called to do more/less based on this practice?

CHAPTER 3

Compassion:
Loving Kindness Prayer

I give you a new commandment, that you love one another.
Just as I have loved you, you also should love one another.

—John 13:34

But I say to you, love your enemies and pray for those who
persecute you. —Matthew 5:44

We human beings are relational creatures. We're linked by complex webs of social connections, some of which we choose and many we don't. Relationships are hard. People are unique and diverse, so we can clash with one another in a multitude of ways. We see this in the many stories and songs depicting relationships. Interpersonal drama is a common theme across all cultures and time periods. Whether it's conflict with our loved ones, insecurity about how others perceive us, or irritation toward people we don't get along with, interpersonal interactions are often a source of stress.

Advice on improving relationships is almost as prevalent as the drama surrounding them. Many self-help trends focus on asserting our own needs to find satisfaction in relationships. Spiritual traditions, by contrast, emphasize finding compassion for the other person. The "Golden Rule" of treating others how you'd like to be treated can be found in almost every spiritual and philosophical tradition. In Christian scripture, the golden rule follows directly after Jesus' command to love our enemies (Luke 6:27–31). This context takes loving others to a more radical level. God instructs us to love *all* people, even those we don't get along with.

Expanding the circle of those we love is no easy task. Compassion requires us to look beyond our hurt and frustration to recognize what we have in common with those we find difficult. We all want and need the same basic things, but our strategies for meeting those needs can look very different. The love God asks us to share with our neighbors and our enemies requires that we remember our similarity even in moments of disagreement and conflict. With practice, this kind of love can become a life-changing spiritual exercise. Compassion not only helps us get along with others, it also shifts our emotional perspective. By focusing on our shared humanity in times of interpersonal stress, we can reduce the impact of anger and resentment by choosing how to respond to these feelings.

The foundation of our compassion is God's unconditional love. Our source for loving others is God's love for us. First John 4:19 makes this path quite clear: we love others *because* God first loved us. Trying to start from our own reserves will never be sustainable, especially when it comes to loving the more difficult people in our lives. True compassion for others must be rooted in the love God offers all people—including ourselves. When we feel and acknowledge God's love for us, we find it easier to approach those difficult people in our lives. The Loving Kindness Prayer helps us draw from the deep well of God's love in order to increase our capacity for loving others.

What Is the Loving Kindness Prayer?

The Loving Kindness Prayer is a structured way to offer blessings for ourselves and others. Instead of focusing on what we don't like about someone, we ground ourselves in God's unconditional love and choose to pray for that person's peace and well-being. We remember our commonality and acknowledge that God's love is the remedy for our shared wounds. The Loving Kindness Prayer challenges us to move beyond superficial "niceness" to a deeper sense of compassion for those around us, as well as for ourselves.

When Jesus teaches us to love our neighbors and our enemies, scripture uses the Greek term *agape*. This type of love is not romantic or even affectionate but describes the attitude of wishing someone well or caring about their well-being. As the Rev. Dr. Martin Luther King Jr. wrote, "We should be happy that he did not say, 'Like your enemies.' It is almost impossible to like some people."[1] King defined liking as sentimental affection but described the love Jesus commands as "creative, redemptive goodwill."[2] This distinction is especially helpful for recognizing that God's charge to love others doesn't mean we'll be free of difficult emotions toward the people we are trying to love. King wrote openly about the difficulty of trying to love white perpetrators of racism and segregation, but he believed it necessary.[3] It is possible, though not easy, to feel angry and hurt by someone but still care about their welfare. *The Loving Kindness Prayer is a tool for reflecting God's radical, redemptive love even toward those who have harmed us.*

The Loving Kindness Prayer outlined in this chapter shares its basic shape with a traditional Buddhist meditation known as *metta*, but it differs in its basic assumptions.[4] The word *metta* roughly translates to loving kindness or compassion, similar to the concept of *agape*. In Buddhism, people practice *metta* meditation to increase their compassion and goodwill toward all beings, with the ultimate goal of achieving enlightenment. The Christian perspective emphasizes God's compassion for us as the foundation of our capacity to love others. The goal of increasing empathy is the same, but the source is different. As Christians we acknowledge the limits of our own capacity to extend kindness and well-being to others. When we feel ourselves struggling to love someone, we can trust that God's infinite *agape* love extends beyond our limitations.

The steps of the Loving Kindness Prayer follow the flow of God's love outlined in scripture.[5] All love is from God, so that's where we start in our attempt to love others. We first acknowledge and receive the love God offers to us, exactly as we are. Once we are in touch with that unconditional *agape* love, we can begin to love ourselves, our neighbors, and the difficult people in our lives. God loves us first, and as we fill up with God's love it can flow through us to those around us.

---

[1] Martin Luther King Jr., *Strength to Love* (San Francisco, CA: Harper & Row, 1963), 37.

[2] King, *Strength to Love*, 37.

[3] King, *Strength to Love*, 37ff.

[4] I present my version of this practice with awareness of and gratitude for the Buddhist lineage in which it developed. Because spiritual practices are often shared freely across traditions out of a common desire to enhance the well-being of all people, I hope and pray that I can do so without causing harm or disrespect to the original tradition.

[5] See John 15:9–17 and 1 John 4:7–21.

The prayer is organized as a series of blessings for people in expanding circles of our lives. It starts with ourselves then widens to people we naturally care about, then to people we may not know well, to people whom we find difficult, and finally to all people. Each section of the prayer offers a blessing for someone to feel God's peace, love, and joy. Using the same blessings for each category helps us to remember we are all God's children and we all need the same things to thrive. The structure of the Loving Kindness Prayer enables us first to tap into the love God offers us, using that love to strengthen our own capacity to love others.

Loving Kindness Prayer in Scripture and Tradition

The Christian commitment to loving others originates with the Sermon on the Mount. Jesus took the well-known commandment "love your neighbor" and broadened it to include loving enemies and praying for persecutors. He contradicted the common assumption at the time that the love command only applied to those within one's own religion or culture.[6] The well-known parable of the good Samaritan in Luke 10 further emphasizes this message that God's directive to love extends beyond cultural boundaries. Loving our neighbors entails much more than caring about the people in our circle of kinship. Jesus challenges us to expand our compassion to anyone in need of care, including those with whom we have conflict.

The early church took Jesus' message seriously. Biblical scholar John Piper has argued that Jesus' command to love enemies was one of the distinctive marks of early Christianity, setting it apart from other traditions that put qualifiers on whom to love.[7] He highlights how early interpretations of Jesus' teaching emphasized concern for both the physical and spiritual well-being of one's enemies, leading up to an attitude of blessing toward them.[8] In the early centuries, when Christians were being actively persecuted for their faith, this ethic led some to martyrdom. Even as they were being tortured and killed, the martyrs prayed for their tormentors, drawing on the example of Jesus' dying prayer: "Forgive them, for they know not what they do."[9] As

---

[6] John Piper, *'Love Your Enemies:' Jesus' Love Command in the Synoptic Gospels and in the Early Christian Paraenesis* (Cambridge, UK: Cambridge University Press, 1979), 91, 128.

[7] Piper, *'Love Your Enemies,'* 64.

[8] Piper, *'Love Your Enemies,'* 129–30.

[9] See, for example, the last words of Stephen in Acts 7:60.

the church continued to grow, Christian writers tried to gain more acceptance within the culture by highlighting their ability to get along with their enemies.[10]

Once Christianity became an established religion, the question of loving others became more of a theological exploration. Christian writers explored the philosophical aspects of what it means to say that God is love or that we are called to love our enemies. Saint Augustine used the concept of love to help explain the relationships between the Father, Son, and Holy Spirit, then drew a parallel between that divine love and the love we share as human beings.[11] Centuries later Thomas Aquinas considered possible objections to Jesus' command to love one's enemies. He argued that "enemies" deserve love because they are fellow humans who share our desire for happiness.[12]

Whenever times of conflict arose, Christian leaders looked to Jesus' teaching on love as a guide for how to respond. Dietrich Bonhoeffer, famous for his role as a faithful Christian witness against Hitler's Nazi regime, highlighted Jesus' command to love enemies as a distinct feature of true discipleship.[13] During the American Civil Rights Movement, Rev. Dr. Martin Luther King Jr. wrote passionately about the love command in his book *The Strength to Love.* "We love our enemies," he wrote, "by realizing that they are not totally bad and that they are not beyond the reach of God's redemptive love."[14] Desmond Tutu likewise built on Jesus' commands to love enemies in his work chairing the Truth and Reconciliation Commission in South Africa after apartheid. "For our nation to heal and become a more humane place," wrote Tutu, "we had to embrace our enemies as well as our

---

[10] For example, Justin Martyr wrote that "we who hated and destroyed one another, and on account of their different manners would not live with men of a different tribe, now, since the coming of Christ, live familiarly with them, and pray for our enemies." *First Apology of Justin Martyr*, chap. 16, Christian Classics Ethereal Library, https://ccel.org/ccel/schaff/anf01/anf01.viii.ii.xiv.html.

[11] Augustine, *De Trinitate*, Christian Classics Ethereal Library, https://ccel.org/ccel/schaff/npnf103.iv.i.html.

[12] Thomas Aquinas, "Treatise on the Theological Virtues" Question 25, Article 8, in *Summa Theologica,* Christian Classics Ethereal Library, https://ccel.org/ccel/aquinas/summa.SS_Q25_A8.html#:~:text=Secondly%20love%20of%20one%27s%20enemies%20may%20mean%20that,the%20love%20given%20to%20our%20neighbor%20in%20general.

[13] Dietrich Bonhoeffer, *The Cost of Discipleship* (New York: Simon & Schuster, 1959), 146–54.

[14] King, *Strength to Love*, 36.

friends."[15] All three recognized that the difficult task of developing compassion for those we consider enemies was a key to overcoming injustice and improving society as a whole.

Why Try the Loving Kindness Prayer?

In addition to the hope of improving the world around us, there are also personal benefits to practicing compassion. We all have people who get under our skin—that coworker who talks too much in meetings or the family member who doesn't respect our boundaries. Sometimes our frustration is rooted in deeper feelings toward someone who has truly harmed us. Other times we're just annoyed by personal pet peeves. Either way, our irritation can build up to the point that it affects our attitude and mood. Often, the more we interact with a difficult person, the more irritable we become.

When I notice my irritation building, my first instinct is to vent to someone I trust. I'm looking for reassurance that my feelings are normal. Venting feels good, and I usually get some validation. But it doesn't solve anything. It doesn't change my relationship with the person I find difficult. I still have to interact with them, and each time I do the same irritations come up again. I start keeping score of all the annoying things that person has done and use that to justify my ongoing resentment. At my worst, I even justify my own unkind words and actions because I've convinced myself the difficult person is to blame.

Learning to love others, especially those difficult people, takes time and practice. We may start by treating others with superficial kindness, only to find that internally we're still stewing. Our thoughts are full of blame and judgment, even if our actions look "nice." We may even turn our negative thoughts on ourselves and criticize our own feelings, which doesn't help. Telling ourselves we *shouldn't* feel so upset doesn't change the fact that we do. All it does is make us feel worse, leaving us with less energy for actually loving other people.

Developing compassion benefits us just as much as the people we're trying to love. Studies show that regular practice of compassion meditations like the Loving Kindness Prayer can decrease anxiety,

---

[15] Desmond Tutu, "Truth and Reconciliation," *Greater Good Magazine,* September 1, 2004, https://greatergood.berkeley.edu/article/item/truth_and_ reconciliation.

increase feelings of calm, and reduce interpersonal conflict.[16] When I practice this prayer regularly, I feel lighter. I'm no longer carrying around a load of resentment or looking for evidence of others' faults. Showing kindness to others feels easier and more sincere when it grows out of prayerful reflection on our common humanity.

Pioneering researcher Kristen Neff has focused on self-compassion—the practice of offering kindness and acceptance to oneself as a way to combat self-criticism and judgment. She highlights the benefits of resilience and self-awareness, as well as the link between self-compassion and deeper, more fulfilling relationships.[17] Compassion for others, as it turns out, is directly tied to compassion for ourselves. Getting better at one also improves our ability to do the other. By tying the two together within the framework of God's infinite compassion for all people, the Loving Kindness Prayer helps us approach both ourselves and the people in our lives with more openness and grace.

Loving our enemies is arguably one of the most difficult things Jesus calls us to do. When we feel hurt or betrayed by someone, our natural impulse is to stew in the feelings of resentment and anger that arise whenever we think of that person. The more energy we give to those difficult emotions, the more prone we are to keep feeling them. The same thing happens when we get upset with ourselves and focus on our own mistakes and limitations. The Loving Kindness Prayer offers a path out of this vicious cycle. Just like strengthening a muscle, we can increase our capacity to feel *agape* love. Daily practice of the Loving Kindness Prayer trains our mind to be more open and compassionate to ourselves and others.

The Loving Kindness Prayer can also be a practical way to prepare ourselves for interactions with difficult people. Rather than steeling ourselves and expecting the worst, the prayer encourages us to start from the foundation of God's love for us. It is out of that unlimited supply of compassion that we draw the strength to be more kind toward those we find difficult. When I've taken the time to practice the Loving Kindness Prayer before facing a challenging

---

[16] See the body of research done by the Center for Compassion and Altruism Research and Education at Stanford (https://ccare.stanford.edu/, accessed April 1, 2024).

[17] Kristen Neff, *Self-Compassion: Stop Beating Yourself Up and Leave Insecurity Behind* (New York: Harper Collins, 2011).

person, I find myself less defensive and more accepting. Compassion has the potential to de-escalate conflict and increase our capacity for kindness.

How to Practice the Loving Kindness Prayer

Take a minute to settle your mind and body and become aware of God's presence. Sit comfortably, take a few deep breaths, and set your intention to connect with God's love. Move through the steps of the prayer slowly, allowing yourself to settle into the feelings of love and compassion. If at any point you feel resistant to offer the prayer for someone, return to step 1 and reconnect with God's deep compassion for you.[18]

1) Begin by focusing on God's love for you.

It may be helpful to picture yourself as a child, embraced by God's compassion and tenderness. Allow this feeling of unconditional love to fill you up as you silently repeat the following phrases several times:

May I feel God's love.

May I feel God's peace.

May I feel God's joy.

2) Picture someone you feel close to.

You can select a family member or close friend—anyone who naturally brings up feelings of care and affection. See that person in your mind, and allow yourself to feel the depth of your love and care for this person. Repeat the prayer several times again for this person:

May they feel God's love.

May they feel God's peace.

May they feel God's joy.

---

[18] If you have experienced significant trauma or are working through an especially painful relationship, please consult a mental health professional about how and when to engage this practice. To focus on your own healing, you may want to limit yourself to using step 1 before trying to expand to showing compassion for others.

3) Picture someone in your life about whom you h neutral feelings.

Select someone you interact with often but don't know very well. This might be a neighbor, a work acquaintance, or the cashier at your local convenience store. Offer your prayer again, silently, a few times for this person:

May they feel God's love.

May they feel God's peace.

May they feel God's joy.

4) Think of a person whom you find difficult.

Here's where things can get harder. Think of someone who annoys you or brings up feelings of frustration. Remind yourself that this person is also a beloved child of God. Picture them in your mind, and offer them the same basic blessings:

May they feel God's love.

May they feel God's peace.

May they feel God's joy.

5) Expand your sense of love to all people in the world.

Remind yourself that God's love extends to all people. Imagine the connections between people all around the world, and offer up this prayer for everyone:

May we all feel God's love.

May we all feel God's peace.

May we all feel God's joy.

As you finish the prayer, spend a minute or so in silence. Observe how you feel, physically and emotionally. Try to carry a sense of openness and compassion into the rest of your day.

Tips for Practicing the Loving Kindness Prayer

Don't judge yourself. If negative emotions arise, remind yourself that these feelings are normal. Return to the first step, and tap into God's unconditional love again. Offer yourself compassion for whatever you are feeling.

Start small. It may be difficult to pray for someone who has hurt you deeply. For step 4, you can select someone you find slightly irritating but not painful. As you practice more and build up a store of compassion, you may find it becomes easier to pray for someone you find more difficult.

Be prepared. If you know you're going to have to interact with a difficult person, practice the Loving Kindness Prayer ahead of time with that person in mind. For brief encounters, you can say the prayer through once right beforehand. For more intense conflicts, repeat the prayer every day for a week or more leading up to the interaction to help maintain your compassionate stance.

Reflection

Once you've had a chance to try the Loving Kindness Prayer a few times, take a moment to reflect using the questions below. You can journal your responses, talk to a friend or spiritual director, or think through them silently.

- What was most challenging for you about the Loving Kindness Prayer?
- What was most rewarding for you?
- How did you select whom to focus on for each section?
- In what ways did this practice affect your daily relationships?
- What, if any, shift did you notice in your overall emotions or attitude?

CHAPTER 4

Mindfulness: Practicing the Presence of God

The Lord your God is with you wherever you go.

—Joshua 1:9b

Have you ever arrived somewhere like work or the grocery store and realized you don't remember getting yourself there? It's easy to go through our days on autopilot, barely noticing where we are or what we're experiencing. So much of our activity is built on habits and routines, leaving our minds free to roam. We run through our to-do lists, review what happened yesterday, or worry about what might go wrong tomorrow. When we're so focused on the past or the future, we often miss what's going on here and now.

Amidst all our daily activities, it's easy to lose sight of our connection to God, who has promised to be present with us always. In theory we know God is present, but we rarely acknowledge this in our day-to-day tasks. We might set aside times of prayer or worship, but in the rest of our activities we carry on as if our faith is irrelevant. Such a disconnect between our daily lives and our spirituality can leave us feeling empty and purposeless. It's easy to forget what really matters and why we do all these things in the first place.

The practice of mindfulness can be an antidote to our mindlessness. It's a way of focusing our attention on our current experience: the thoughts, emotions, and sensations happening in this moment. Such connection with the here and now can help us become aware of the reality of God's presence around and within us. Recognition of this divine presence takes practice—reminding ourselves over and over to let go of our distractions and simply be with God. As we develop our capacity to stay present, we increase our ability to see God's Spirit at work all around us in each moment.

Practicing the Presence of God is a way of using mindfulness to increase our awareness of God in daily activities. It's a way of recognizing that even our mundane chores can be acts of faith, infused with spiritual purpose. Each task we complete can be an offering and a prayer. Each activity becomes a spiritual practice as we acknowledge God's presence alongside us. Such awareness shifts our perspective and builds our sense of gratitude and connection to the Creator and Source of all life.

What Is Practicing the Presence of God?

Practicing the Presence of God means actively attending to God's presence during daily tasks. This can be done during any activity: taking a shower, folding laundry, running errands, or driving to work. Any of these tasks can become a spiritual practice when carried out with awareness of our relationship to God. It's as if we're inviting God into the nitty-gritty details of our life, only to realize God is already there, keeping us company as we go about our day.

Acknowledging God's presence may seem like a simple concept, but it can be surprisingly difficult to practice. We are creatures of habit, easily distracted by all the thoughts and worries that normally fill our minds. Practicing the Presence of God doesn't require perfect focus; distraction is inevitable. Instead, it's an invitation to continually redirect our attention back to what we're doing in the present moment and acknowledge God's presence with us. The tools and strategies of mindfulness, an increasingly popular mental health tool, can help us improve our capacity for this practice.

Jon Kabat Zinn, founder of Mindfulness-Based Stress Reduction, describes mindfulness as "paying attention in a particular way, on purpose, in the present moment, and nonjudgmentally."[1] Each aspect of this definition helps clarify how we can better experience God's presence in daily life.

Paying attention requires focus and awareness. It's the opposite of being on "autopilot" mode. We use our senses to stay fully awake to the details of the world around us, as well our

---

[1] "Jon Kabat-Zinn: Defining Mindfulness," *Mindful*, January 11, 2017, https://www.mindful.org/jon-kabat-zinn-defining-mindfulness/.

internal experiences. We want to offer God the same kind of attention we would give to a beloved friend—setting aside distractions so we can enjoy the time together.[2]

On purpose implies that this is an intentional choice. There are plenty of other things we could pay attention to, but we are choosing to attend to God's presence. Our purposefulness sets this time apart as a spiritual practice and not just another mindless task.

In the present moment reminds us to let go of the past and the future so we can experience fully what it's like to be with God right now. There are times when we need to reflect back or plan ahead. But our relationship with God is in the present. We need to stay in this moment to realize fully that God is here with us.

Nonjudgmentally describes an attitude free of expectations or evaluation. We don't set goals for our time with God: we simply experience it. This requires letting go of our worries about whether we're "doing it right." Even when distractions pull our attention away, we don't need to judge ourselves. It's enough to notice that our minds have wandered and to remind ourselves gently of our intention to be present with God.

Another concept from secular mindfulness training that can aid our awareness of the Presence of God is known as *beginner's mind*. This is the idea of approaching everyday activities as if we're experiencing them for the first time. We let go of assumptions and engage our curiosity to see what we might learn here and now. We experience a sense of childlike awe and wonder reminiscent of Jesus' words to his disciples in Matthew 18:3: "Unless you change and become like children, you will never enter the kingdom of heaven." Practicing the Presence of God is an invitation to apply childlike enthusiasm to our everyday activities.

---

[2] Simone Weil famously wrote, "Attention, taken to its highest degree, is the same thing as prayer. It presupposes faith and love. Absolutely unmixed attention is prayer." *Gravity and Grace*, quoted in Maria Popova, "Simone Weil on Attention and Grace," *The Marginalian*, August 19, 2015, https://www.themarginalian.org/2015/08/19/simone-weil-attention-gravity-and-grace/.

Mindful attention helps us connect to the deeper reality beneath our busy, distracted lives. In all that we do, God is with us. In every moment, we are already connected to the divine source of life. Each activity becomes an opportunity to root ourselves more deeply in this truth. Practicing the Presence of God means acknowledging the spiritual nature of our daily existence.

Practicing the Presence of God in Scripture and Tradition

In the book of Exodus, when Moses asked God for a name to tell the Israelites who sent him, God's reply expresses a profound truth: "I am who I am." God's identity is life itself, existence, the One who is. It's hard for our human minds to grasp this all-encompassing reality of God, yet we glimpse it in our moments of spiritual connection. The history of faith recounts a multitude of ways people have experienced God's presence throughout their everyday lives. The Psalms are a great example of acknowledging God through the ups and downs of human experience. Psalm 139 speaks of the powerful intimacy of God, who knew us before we were born and whose penetrating presence is found wherever we turn. Throughout scripture God promises always to be with us.[3]

Christian writings extend the invitation to recognize God in all aspects of life. First Thessalonians 5:16–18 advises believers to "rejoice always, pray without ceasing, give thanks in all circumstances." People of faith across the centuries have attempted to clarify the meaning of this call to "unceasing prayer." Saint Augustine in the fourth century described it as an "inward kind of prayer … which is the desire of the heart."[4] He highlighted our constant yearning for God that motivates us to live in accordance with God's teaching. Centuries later, Dutch priest and writer Henri Nouwen wrote that unceasing prayer requires us to "think and live in the presence of God" rather than trying to restrict God only to the pious parts of ourselves.[5] Unceasing prayer does not mean we must spend every waking minute in verbal dialogue with God. It is an invitation to increase our awareness of the divine

---

[3] See Deuteronomy 31:6, Isaiah 41:10, and Matthew 28:20.

[4] Augustine, *Expositions on the Psalms*, trans. J.E. Tweed, edited by Kevin Knight for New Advent, 38:13, https://www.newadvent.org/fathers/1801038.htm.

[5] Henri Nouwen, "How to (Actually) Pray without Ceasing," *America: The Jesuit Review*, January 24, 2022, https://www.americamagazine.org/faith/2022/01/24/henri-nouwen-prayer-unceasing-242269.

Presence that is always with us. Each moment is a new opportunity to experience the joy and gratitude that arise from our awareness of God.

Monastic traditions have tied the call to unceasing prayer with the daily rhythms of work and communal life. The Latin phrase *ora et labora*, meaning "pray and work," is often associated with the monastic Rule of St. Benedict. The Rule outlines the expectations for both set times of daily prayer as well as periods of physical labor, often attending to the care and upkeep of the community.[6] Over time the Latin motto evolved into a more nuanced statement: *laborare est orare*, or "to work is to pray." This shift expresses a recognition that God is to be sought and found in the mundane tasks of life as well as the sacred ones.

Writings from the seventeenth and eighteenth centuries made explicit the spiritual potential of mindfully engaging in daily tasks. A short book titled *The Practice of the Presence of God* recounts the wisdom of an uneducated monk known as Brother Lawrence who worked as a cook and sandal maker at a Carmelite monastery in France. As one of his fellow monks narrates: "The most excellent method he had found of going to God was that of doing our common business without any view of pleasing [people], and (as far as we are capable) purely for the love of God. … His prayer was nothing else but a sense of the presence of God."[7] Similarly, French Jesuit priest Jean-Pierre de Caussade described the value of communing with God through menial tasks. In his book *The Sacrament of the Present Moment*, he wrote, "To discover God in the smallest and most ordinary things, as well as in the greatest, is to possess a rare and sublime faith."[8] Both Brother Lawrence and de Caussade recognized that if God is everywhere, people of faith can experience God's presence in each moment.

In the twentieth century modern existential angst led to explorations of how God's transcendent presence could be known by finite human experience. Paul Tillich, a German theologian who was exiled to the U.S. during the Nazi regime, famously described God as "the Ground of Being." In his book *The Courage to Be*, he argued that disconnection from this source of our life and being was the ultimate

---

[6] Timothy Fry, ed., *The Rule of St. Benedict in English* (Collegeville, MN: The Liturgical Press, 1982), 69.

[7] Brother Lawrence, *The Practice of the Presence of God with Spiritual Maxims*, trans. Fleming H. Revell (Grand Rapids: Baker Publishing Group, 1967), 26.

[8] Jean-Pierre de Caussade, *The Sacrament of the Present Moment*, trans. Kitty Muggeridge (San Francisco, CA: Harper & Row, 1966), 64.

˜ human anxiety.[9] Tillich and other existential theologians ˷ Rudolf Bultmann and Karl Rahner sought to understand how human beings could truly know and reconnect to the source of all existence when our language and images for God are so limited. Their heady philosophical explorations ultimately hearken back to God's answer to Moses: "I am who I am." If God is the ground of our very being, then Practicing the Presence of God is a way to experience that transcendence by allowing ourselves to be, just as we are, in the present moment.

Why Try Practicing the Presence of God?

Mindfulness may sound like a trendy word, but its popularity speaks to the powerful benefits found in focusing on the present moment. We put so much mental energy into either revisiting the past or preparing for the future that we miss out on opportunities for joy right now. It's easy to get caught up in old feelings of regret or consumed by anxiety about the future, but this takes a toll on our mental health and obscures our connection to God.

I remember vividly the moment I first experienced this truth. I was in college, walking across campus from one class to another. My mind was caught up in its usual stream of worrying and planning, and I was barely aware of where I was going. Suddenly I was struck by a strong gust of spring wind. The warmth of the air shook me loose from my thoughts. I noticed the sunshine and the blue sky. I felt my feet hitting the ground with each step. I felt suddenly alive and profoundly aware of God's presence walking with me. My anxieties seemed smaller in the light of this powerful connection.

Brain imaging studies indicate that practicing mindfulness can make lasting changes in our wiring. It strengthens the areas of the brain that promote learning, creativity, and compassion, while decreasing activity in brain areas related to anxiety and stress responses.[10] Centuries before any of this research was even possible, Brother Lawrence had figured out that the key to finding joy and contentment in daily life was to stay in the moment and find meaning in every task. Recognition of God's presence builds a deeper connection to our spiritual foundation, which can buffer us against the stresses of daily life.

---

[9] Daniel J. Peterson, *Tillich: A Brief Overview of the Life and Writings of Paul Tillich* (Minneapolis, MN: Lutheran University Press, 2013).

[10] See the research of Sara Lazar at https://scholar.harvard.edu/sara_lazar.

Mindfulness is like turning on a light in a dark room. Mindfulness helps us to understand our current situation and to navigate our lives with more clarity. Without awareness, we can lose sight of where we are and where we're going. In his book *Full Catastrophe Living*, Jon Kabat-Zinn suggests this is why mindfulness is so effective in managing stress: "As soon as you intentionally bring awareness to what is going on in a stressful situation, you have already changed that situation dramatically."[11] Seeing our experience as it is gives us the opportunity to respond with more freedom. Personal and spiritual growth are only possible when we see the reality before us and acknowledge the choices God has given us in each moment.

Practicing the Presence of God as a spiritual discipline can also increase our experience of joy and gratitude. When we learn to release our expectations and judgments, we stop comparing our current situation to what we think it should be. Accepting reality as it is opens us to feel our authentic emotions, including appreciation for the simple experiences that bring joy to our days. We start to notice the tiny rainbows in the soap bubbles as we wash the dishes instead of wishing there were fewer dirty plates. We marvel at the shapes of the clouds instead of worrying whether it will rain. We enjoy a favorite song while we sit in traffic rather than ruminating on how long we've been stuck there. Research has shown that attitudes of acceptance and non-judgment are the elements of mindfulness that most increase pleasant emotions.[12] When we add awareness of the Creator who gifted us with these moments of joy, our mindfulness becomes a prayer of gratitude and praise.

Despite what our busy, anxious minds may tell us, multitasking and overanalyzing are not going to help us feel secure and grounded. As de Caussade wrote, "Our souls can only be truly nourished, strengthened, enriched and sanctified by the bounty of the present moment."[13] Practicing the Presence of God can help us turn even the simplest task into a powerful spiritual practice by paying attention to God, who is the ever present source of our well-being.

---

[11] Jon Kabat-Zinn, *Full Catastrophe Living: Using the Wisdom of Your Body and Mind to Face Stress, Pain, and Illness*, rev. ed. (New York: Bantam, 2013), 336.

[12] Melanie Greenberg, "The Surprising Reason Mindfulness Makes You Happier," *Psychology Today*, January 27, 2020, https://www.psychologytoday.com/us/blog/the-mindful-self-express/202001/the-surprising-reason-mindfulness-makes-you-happier.

[13] Caussade, *Sacrament*, 81.

How to Practice the Presence of God

Select an everyday activity to be your spiritual practice. Feel free to use the same task each day or try a variety. The key is to be intentional and not on autopilot. Try not to multitask; focus your full attention on this one activity.

1) Start with purpose.

Take a moment before you begin to remind yourself of your intention to Practice the Presence of God. This activity may be a necessary chore, but it is also a prayer. Whatever you plan to do, you will do it in the Presence of God.

2) Acknowledge God's presence.

As you begin your task, remind yourself that God is already present with you. It may help to imagine God physically standing or sitting beside you, like a friend keeping you company. You can offer a word of greeting if you wish or simply smile as you might to a loved one as you share an activity together.

3) Explore your senses.

Pay attention to the physical sensations of your task. What do you see? Hear? Smell? Taste? Touch? Your five senses can help you stay focused on the present moment. This can be especially helpful if you feel distracted. Whenever you notice your mind wandering, return to the physical sensations and to your awareness of God's presence alongside you.

4) Be kind to yourself.

Accept your current experience without judgment. Let go of expectations for how you should think or feel. If criticism arises in your mind, simply notice it and return to your awareness of the task. Allow yourself to receive the present moment just as it is.

5) End with gratitude.

At the completion of your task, thank God for keeping you company. Reflect on any moments of enjoyment that arose during the practice, and allow gratitude to fill you. If any other thoughts or concerns came to mind during your practice, take a moment to offer them to God in prayer.

Tips for Practicing the Presence of God

Keep trying. Distraction is inevitable. Notice when it happens, but don't get hung up on it. Remind yourself that the intention is to spend time with God, not to achieve perfect spiritual focus. It's called *practicing* for a reason!

Minimize interruptions. As best you can, limit any outside disruptions that will make it harder to stay present. Turn off the notifications on your phone. Don't leave the TV or radio playing. Let others around you know you're having some "quiet time" (or save your practice for activities you can do alone).

Make it a gift. If you're finding your activity unpleasant or boring, remind yourself that you're offering it to God as a spiritual practice. Just as you might do a chore as a favor for a loved one, let this be a gift to God. Chistian writer and activist Jim Forest recounts a conversation in which a Buddhist mindfulness teacher encouraged him to "wash every dish as if it were the baby Jesus."[14]

Reflection

Once you've had a chance to try Practicing the Presence of God, take a moment to reflect using the questions below. You can journal your responses, talk to a friend or spiritual director, or think through them silently.

- Which activity or activities did you choose to Practice the Presence of God?

- Which physical sensations did you observe during the practice?

- What was different about doing your task as a spiritual practice?

- Was there a particular moment from the practice that stands out in your mind? Why?

- What did you find challenging about Practicing the Presence of God?

- During which other activities would you like to try Practicing the Presence of God?

<hr>

[14] Jim Forest, *The Road to Emmaus: Pilgrimage as Way of Life* (Maryknoll, NY: Orbis Books, 2007), 17.

CHAPTER 5

Rest: Sabbath

Six days you shall labor and do all your work. But the seventh day is a sabbath to the Lord your God; you shall not do any work. —Exodus 20:9–10

The Energizer Bunny has become a cultural icon of productivity. We use the name as a compliment for those who push themselves to keep going when the rest of us wear out. We love the idea of something that goes forever, without stopping. We idolize this ideal of endless energy and nonstop production, but it's an impossible standard. Human beings are not perpetual motion machines. We are living, breathing creatures who need rest.

The danger of our productivity culture lies in its indifference to human needs. That culture has conditioned us to prioritize efficiency without considering the cost. Whether it's our own stress-induced medical problems or the well-being of factory workers around the world, someone is usually paying the price when we expect everything to be better, faster, and more. When we value the product over the people who create it, something is off balance.

Spiritual traditions have long upheld the value of humanity over production. Faith teaches us to find purpose and meaning in more than just our work. Our rest and play say just as much, if not more, about who we are. Maintaining our humanity requires protecting time for relationships, relaxation, and rest. We need this downtime ourselves, and we also owe it to others. The goods and services we enjoy always come at the cost of someone else's labor. Justice requires that those laborers also have opportunity for rest.

The Ten Commandments explicitly name rest as a requirement for human life. It's not a suggestion but a command. God seems to recognize and preempt our tendency to idolize productivity. It reminds me of trying to enforce bedtime for my children. They often protest that they're not tired, but I know they need the rest. God likewise recognizes what we need even when we struggle to see it ourselves. The command to rest stands in direct contrast to the cultural pressures to stay busy.

Rest is not always an easy thing to find. Many of us carry multiple loads of financial and caregiving burdens that can't be easily set aside. Even for those with the privilege of free time, there's pressure to "make the most of it," turning leisure activities into competitive marks of achievement. It takes conscious commitment and sacrifice to truly rest. When we engage the practice of Sabbath rest, we consciously invest time in rejuvenating our minds and bodies. We set aside time as an offering to God, who invites us to find rest for our weary souls.

What is Sabbath?

You may have heard the word Sabbath in church or if you're familiar with Jewish traditions. It refers to setting aside one day a week as holy, or separate, from the other working days. The word itself literally means rest, but we can easily forget this when we focus on Sabbath as something we have to practice. Sabbath is not about doing more or adding extra spiritual things. *What makes Sabbath holy is allowing ourselves to rest.* Resting is not something our culture values, so we must be intentional about building it into our lives.

Jewish scholar Abraham Heschel describes the Sabbath as a practice of sanctifying time, or making time holy.[1] "Mundane" is the opposite of holy. All those ordinary, earthly things that fill so much of our days leave little room for experiencing what we hold sacred. Heschel explains the Jewish perspective of Sabbath as a taste of eternity, "an example of the world to come."[2] The spiritual qualities of peace, well-being, and connection that we long for are accessible to us through the practice of Sabbath rest.

From a practical standpoint, Sabbath can be a kind of intermission—a pause between the busy acts of our daily life. It's a time to stretch our metaphorical legs so we can return to our obligations

---

[1] Abraham Heschel, *The Sabbath: Its Meaning for Modern Man* (New York: Farrar, Straus, and Young, 1951).

[2] Heschel, *The Sabbath*, 73.

with more energy and focus. Having a designated time to attend to the basic needs of our mind and body ensures that we don't keep shoving them to the side in favor of endless pressing obligations. The obligations will still be there when we return, but we're better able to manage them after we take time to rest.

For those in caregiving roles, the invitation to Sabbath rest is an opportunity for self-care. The demands of caring for children, aging parents, partners with chronic illness, or anyone else who depends on us can feel unrelenting. Taking time for ourselves often brings up feelings of guilt that we are prioritizing our own needs over the needs of those we care for. And yet God calls us to rest. Sabbath is a reminder that we can't run nonstop. Regular periods of rest from the constant needs of others are crucial to our well-being. If God, who is responsible for all creation, can take a day of rest, then we can too. Caring for others requires that we sustain ourselves, and the gift of Sabbath reminds us that we, too, deserve care.

The core of Sabbath rest is recognizing that our value lies in who we are, not what we do. God's love is not contingent on our accomplishments. Even when we're doing nothing, God sees us as worthy and beloved. Jesus extended an invitation for all who are weary to come and find rest.[3] Sabbath is our conscious response to that invitation—a response of choosing to stop *doing* and instead simply to *be* with God. Sabbath practice helps us experience spiritual connection.

Sabbath rest can take many forms. Physical rest and sleep help restore our bodies, while hobbies and creative expression can nourish our souls. Some people may find it rejuvenating to spend time with friends and family, while others are more restored by time alone. Rest may look very different for each of us, but it shouldn't feel like work. Instead of another task to be accomplished, Sabbath is a gift to be enjoyed.

Sabbath in Scripture and Tradition

Sabbath is as old as creation itself. Scripture tells us God created the world in six days, and on the seventh day God rested. When the commandment to "honor the sabbath day" was first given to Moses, it was directly related to this day of rest at creation.[4] If God rested after creating the universe, there must be something holy and beneficial

---

[3] Matthew 11:28.
[4] Exodus 20:8–11.

about rest. In Jewish tradition, Sabbath takes place on the seventh day of the week in accordance with the seven days of creation. It begins at sundown Friday evening and continues through sundown Saturday. The type of work prohibited on this day extends beyond gainful employment to encompass household labor and operating mechanical equipment. Activities such as lighting candles, cooking food, driving cars, and even pushing elevator buttons may constitute "work" that ought not be done on the Sabbath.

Hebrew Scripture also ties the Sabbath commandment to the freedom of the Israelites from slavery in Egypt.[5] God's rest is set in clear opposition to dehumanizing oppression and forced labor. Sabbath practices are prescribed every seven days, every seven years, and every forty-nine (seven times seven) years.[6] Known as the Sabbath Year and Year of Jubilee, these additional Sabbath laws highlight the collective nature of God's invitation to rest. In the Sabbath Year, the land is allowed to rest from farming and those working off debts are granted a clean slate. In the Year of Jubilee, all land returns to its original family of ownership. These practices indicate that Sabbath rest is a form of restoration for the whole community, particularly the most vulnerable. Biblical scholar Richard Lowry highlights the social and environmental justice implications of the Sabbath Year and Year of Jubilee, noting that they also provide a theological reminder that God liberates land and people from the tyranny of human ownership.[7]

Christian adaptations of Sabbath practice developed in the early years of the church. As the early Christians negotiated how to balance their Jewish roots with the inclusion of non-Jewish believers, they developed a practice of worshipping on Sundays in honor of Jesus' resurrection on a Sunday. Over time this Sunday worship came to be understood to be a Christian expression of God's command to take a Sabbath rest. Various interpretations of Christian Sabbath practices have evolved since then. American Puritan heritage taught that nearly all activity was forbidden on Sundays, a belief that manifested in so-called "blue laws" forbidding particular activities and business transactions on Sundays in some states. In the nineteenth century founders of the Seventh-day Adventist Church drew on literal

---

[5] Deuteronomy 5:12–15.

[6] Exodus 23:10–11; Deuteronomy 15:1–18; Leviticus 25:1–7, 18–24.

[7] Richard H. Lowery, *Sabbath and Jubilee* (St. Louis, MO: Chalice Press, 2000), 76–77.

interpretations of the Sabbath commandment to argue for Christian observance of Sabbath on Saturdays rather than Sundays.

In response to such legalistic portrayals of Sabbath, many contemporary churches have stopped talking about it all together and have instead given in to the culture of busyness. Rather than discourage activity, churches often seek to compete by showcasing their vast array of programs. In addition to Sunday worship services, there are activities throughout the week: education classes, youth group meetings, committee meetings, fundraisers, book clubs, and any number of other busy activities. There can be great value in many of these, but when layered upon all the other commitments in our lives they leave little room for rest. The church continues to struggle with how to preserve the value of Sabbath in the face of constant competition for our time and attention.

Returning to the revolutionary roots of Sabbath provides an avenue for appreciating its relevance today. In his book *Sabbath as Resistance* biblical scholar Walter Bruggeman argues that the Sabbath commandment functions as an antidote to the existential anxiety of our contemporary life.[8] He offers slavery in Egypt as a metaphor for our commodity-driven society and suggests that Sabbath practice both resists the anxiety-inducing pressures and offers a clear alternative: "The alternative on offer is the awareness and practice of the claim that we are situated on the receiving end of the gifts of God."[9] Meaningful rest is not something we can produce; it is something we are blessed to receive.

Why Try Practicing Sabbath?

The benefits of rest may seem obvious, but we often struggle to recognize our own needs. Pushing ourselves to do more and more creates a constant sense of anxiety. Without rest, the anxiety weighs on our minds, drains our spirits, and eventually takes a toll on our physical health. The command to practice Sabbath is a loving reminder from God that it's good to take a break.

Popular psychology highlights the need for different types of rest.[10] Sleep deprivation has been studied in depth and is linked to

---

[8] Walter Brueggemann, *Sabbath as Resistance: Saying No to the Culture of Now* (Louisville, KY: Westminster John Knox, 2014).

[9] Brueggemann, *Sabbath as Resistance*, xiv.

[10] See, for example, Claudia Skowron, "The 7 Kinds of Rest You Actually Need," *Psychology Today*, December 21, 2022, https://www.psychologytoday.com/us/blog/a-different-kind-of-therapy/202212/the-7-kinds-of-rest-you-need-to-actually-feel-rejuvenated.

difficulties with mood, memory, immune system, weight, balance, and numerous other physical and mental health conditions.[11] But rest is more than just sleep. Even when we're awake our bodies and minds need downtime to help us process and recover from periods of intense activity. It's why most physical exercise regimens have built-in rest days to allow muscles to rebuild. Our mental and emotional systems work the same way: we need breaks to help integrate the results of our labor.

When I feel overwhelmed, I often worry that resting will only put me further behind on my to-do list. With practice I've learned I'm much more productive after I give myself a break. Periods of intense productivity create a stress response in our bodies that can build up over time. Taking breaks allows that stress level to ease so we can come back to equilibrium. Once the mind and body are recharged, we have more resources to work with for the next task. Creativity flows more freely, and we can focus better on what needs to get done.

In recent decades there has been some buzz around the idea of a "Tech Sabbath."[12] We're increasingly aware of the psychological and behavioral impact of screen-based technology on our lives. Our devices have an addictive quality that can leave us feeling beholden to them. Their ubiquitousness leads to an expectation of constant availability. It's hard to keep boundaries between our work, home, and social lives. Christian educators Paul Patton and Robert Woods explore the impact of digital culture on our ability to experience spiritual growth in their book *Everyday Sabbath*. They highlight the qualities of intentionality, interiority, and identity as keys to practicing Sabbath rest in a tech-focused world.[13] Sabbath rest offers a chance to grow these spiritual qualities rather than letting our devices command our time.

Rest also provides healthy soil in which our relationships can grow. When we're constantly busy, there is little time to enjoy the company of

[11] Cleveland Clinic, "Here's What Happens When You Don't Get Enough Sleep," *Health Essentials,* May 29, 2024, https://health.clevelandclinic.org/happens-body-dont-get-enough-sleep.

[12] A few examples: Brett & Kate McKay, "On the Seventh Day, We Unplug: How and Why to Take a Tech Sabbath"; *Art of Manliness*, May 20, 2014, updated July 2, 2023, https://www.artofmanliness.com/character/advice/tech-sabbath; Austin Considine, "And on the Sabbath, the iPhones Shall Rest," *The New York Times*, March 17, 2010, https://www.nytimes.com/2010/03/18/fashion/18sabbath.html.

[13] Paul D. Patton and Robert H. Woods Jr., *Everyday Sabbath: How to Lead Your Dance with Media and Technology in Mindful and Sacred Ways* (Eugene, OR: Cascade Books, 2021), xli.

our loved ones. And even when we're with them physically, our minds are often distracted by everything we need to get done. Spending time together without the pressure of scheduled activities or goal-oriented tasks makes space for us to connect more deeply with one another. For those of us who are introverted, we can reach a level of social burnout that makes it hard to engage fully with others even when we want to. Taking time to rest in whatever way is most nourishing can fill our emotional tank so we have more to offer our friends and family.

None of us can live without rest. God created us this way. Patterns of activity and dormancy are built into all of creation. Nature always follows seasons of growth and production with seasons of rest and rebuilding. As human creatures we need the daily rhythm of wakefulness and sleep, as well as the weekly rhythm of work and rest. We need regular breaks from the demands we place on ourselves and on the world around us. Sabbath is a practice that reinforces this natural balance, keeping us in touch with the rhythms of God's creation.

How to Practice Sabbath

Since Sabbath rest is a gift from God, our primary task is to make space for receiving it. Rather than focusing on a list of specific prohibitions, consider what you might need to set aside. What would help you create room for rest in your life? You can easily adapt the following steps to your unique needs and preferences.

1) Set a Sabbath schedule.

Choose a realistic block of time to set aside every week. Saturday and Sunday are the traditional options, but your Sabbath can be whatever day you want. It doesn't even have to be a whole day, but meaningful rest will take more than just a few minutes. Put the time on your calendar so you don't accidentally schedule something else then.

2) Unplug.

Turn off or put away any devices that keep you tied to work and other demands. Use automatic responses or let people know ahead of time that you'll be unavailable. If being at home reminds you of everything you need to get done around the house, go somewhere else where you can really disconnect for a Sabbath. If your mental to-do list distracts you during your time of Sabbath, write it down or make a plan for when you will get things done later so you can fully enjoy your rest now. Give yourself a break from thinking about work as well as from doing it.

3) Enjoy your rest.

Spend time doing things that help you feel rested and restored. Take a nap if that sounds good, or go for a walk outside. Allow yourself options. Be playful and creative. Connect with God, nature, and your loved ones. Engage the parts of yourself that don't get much attention the rest of the week.

Tips for Practicing Sabbath

Try not to multi-task. Do one thing at a time. Let yourself be fully present to receive the gift of rest and truly enjoy your Sabbath time.

Avoid bingeing. Feel free to enjoy your favorite treats or watch your favorite shows during your Sabbath, but if you find yourself overdoing it that may be a sign that something else is off balance. Bingeing is usually reactive, while Sabbath rest is proactive.

Rest together. Make an agreement with your family or friends to try a group Sabbath time. Decide together what the expectations will be in terms of frequency, length, and what types of activities you'll enjoy during your shared Sabbath.

Reflection

Once you've had a chance to take a regular Sabbath for a few weeks, spend a moment reflecting on the questions below. You can journal your responses, talk to a friend or spiritual director, or think through them silently.

- How did you build Sabbath rest into your week?
- What did you notice during your Sabbath time?
- In what ways did you experience rest and rejuvenation?
- Did anything get in the way of your ability to rest?
- How might you continue to practice Sabbath rest?

CHAPTER 6

Grounding: Breath Prayer

*The Spirit of God has made me, and the breath of the
Almighty gives me life.*   —Job 33:4

There are a million ways we can feel overwhelmed. Physical
exhaustion, emotional intensity, mental stress, and sensory overload
can all make us feel as if we've hit our limit. When life becomes hectic,
we can experience a sense of disconnection. We may lose track of
important information or fail to notice our basic needs for food and
rest. Often we act on habits and impulses without thinking about
the consequences.

It's also hard to connect with others when we're overwhelmed.
We may feel like zombies, going through the motions but unable
to really engage. When we're burnt out and checked out, there's no
energy left for our relationships, even our relationship with God. We
find ourselves distant from our sources of support and connection
precisely when we need them most.

Common advice for feeling overwhelmed is to stop and take a
deep breath. I use it so much with my children that they parrot it back
at me when I'm getting visibly frustrated: "Mommy, do you need to
take a breath?" Breathing is a surprisingly effective tool for cutting
through the chaos and giving ourselves a chance to pause. We're
breathing twenty-four hours a day, seven days a week. That constant
rhythm of inhale and exhale can ground us in the moment and help
us reconnect to ourselves and those around us.

Breath has deep cultural symbolism as the source of life. It is
foundational to keeping our bodies alive. It also signifies the vitality
of our spirit. Breath can express emotion and intimacy, as well as

physical vigor. We use our breath to speak, cry, laugh, and sing. In the biblical story of creation, God *breathes* life into the clay. This breath of life distinguishes humans from the other animals. Breath is our direct connection to God's Spirit.

When we lose track of our connection to the life-giving Spirit of God, grounding ourselves with our breath can help us reorient ourselves. Each time we breathe in and out, we can acknowledge the source of our life. By using our physical breath as a form of prayer, we can tangibly experience our relationship to the Creator. Breath Prayer allows us to focus and reconnect.

What Is Breath Prayer?

Breath Prayer is exactly what it sounds like: using your breath as a form of prayer. It can be as simple as noticing you are breathing and reminding yourself God is with you. Breath is one of the most common ways the Bible describes the link between God the Creator and us as God's creatures. It's therefore fitting to use our breath intentionally as a tool for connecting to God.

True connection—with God, ourselves, or anyone else—requires us to be fully present to our own experience. We need a way to anchor ourselves amidst the whirlwind of thoughts, feelings, and pressures that fill our hectic lives. *The concept of grounding refers to staying rooted, being "down to earth" and aware of our surroundings.* It's the opposite of dissociation. Breath Prayer is a type of grounding practice that helps us stay present in our bodies. It provides both physical and spiritual stability.

Breath Prayer is extremely flexible. All it requires is inhaling, exhaling, and desiring connection with God. Words aren't necessary, but some people find it helpful to pair silent words or phrases to each inhale and exhale. For example, think *grace* as you breathe in and *peace* as you breathe out. Another option is combining your preferred name for God with your deepest spiritual longing to create a short phrase you can repeat: for example, "Holy One, send me peace."[1] Visual images such as a wave that rises and falls with each breath can also be helpful. Often the physical sensations of air filling your lungs and releasing can be enough to keep your attention focused.

---

[1] Ron DelBene recommends using this method to develop a consistent breath prayer of six to eight syllables for ease of repetition: *The Breath of Life: A Simple Way to Pray* (Nashville, TN: Upper Room Books, 1992), 40–41.

Breath Prayer is different from meditation or Centering Prayer. There is no set length of time or formal structure. It can last for a single round of breath or continue as long as it takes to feel a sense of grounding in God's presence. You simply breathe in and out, allowing yourself to feel God's Spirit sustaining you. This can happen at any point in your day, whether it's the middle of a stressful meeting or in bed as you prepare to fall asleep. Your breath is always with you, and God is always available.

The goal of Breath Prayer is to pause the commotion of our lives and remember who we are. Wherever we go, whatever we are doing, we are infused with the Spirit of God. The Creator breathes life into us each moment. Much like the air that surrounds us, God is always present to nourish and support us. That can be easy to take for granted, but when life becomes overwhelming we can return to our foundation. Breath Prayer gives us a chance to slow down, check in, and remember what really matters. With each breath, we reconnect to the divine source of our life and strength.

Breath Prayer in Scripture and Tradition

The word for "breath" in the Hebrew scriptures is also the word for "spirit." When the creation story in Genesis describes the Spirit of God hovering over the waters, it conveys a picture of God's breath blowing gently across the world before giving it shape.[2] The breath imagery continues as God breathes life into the dusty clay to create Adam, the first human.[3] Throughout scripture, breath is connected to the life-giving Spirit of God. In the Gospel of John, Jesus breathes on the disciples to convey the gift of the Holy Spirit; and at Pentecost that Spirit blows in with a mighty rush of air.[4]

After Pentecost the church continued to grow and expand throughout the Roman Empire. New believers who had no background in the Jewish scriptures struggled to understand the idea of God's Spirit and how it related to Jesus, the Son of God. Saint Basil the Great used the Hebrew imagery of spirit/breath to help clarify. He suggested that just as Jesus is the *Word* of God, the Holy Spirit is the *Breath* of God.[5] He and several other early theologians pointed

---

[2] Genesis 1:2.

[3] Genesis 2:7.

[4] John 20:22; Acts 2:1–4.

[5] Denis Edwards, *Breath of Life: A Theology of the Creator Spirit* (Maryknoll, NY: Orbis Books, 2004), 26.

to Psalm 33:6 as a descriptor of how the Word and Breath worked together in the creation of the world: "By the word of the Lord the heavens were made, and all their host by the breath of his mouth." We get an image of the Holy Spirit as the breath with which God speaks creation into being.

The rich imagery of breath recurs throughout centuries of Christian writings, artwork, and especially music. Numerous popular hymns depict breath as a link between God and humanity. The second verse of Charles Wesley's "Love Divine, All Loves Excelling," written in 1747, asks God to *Breathe, O breathe thy loving Spirit into every troubled breast.* A similar refrain appears in the prayerful hymn "Breathe on Me, Breath of God," written by Edwin Hatch in 1878. The contemporary praise song "Breathe," by Marie Barnett, builds on this tradition, depicting God's presence as the very air we breathe. Breath provides a powerfully embodied understanding of our connection to God's Spirit. Generations of people of faith have cherished this imagery.

In recent years there has been renewed interest in breath as a tool for prayer. Richard Rohr, Franciscan priest and founder of the Center for Action and Contemplation, promotes a Breath Prayer using the divine name, Yahweh, that was given to Moses from the burning bush.[6] He cites a rabbi who taught him that the consonants of the name, Y-H-W-H, form the sound of breathing in and out, such that we are constantly calling on God with each breath that we take. In a video explaining this revelation, Rohr breathes into the microphone to demonstrate this simple but profound Breath Prayer.[7] He highlights the universal quality of this prayer: it has been breathed by every living person around the world.

Holy Spirit imagery ties breath to the mysterious connectedness of all living beings. John 3:8 reminds us the Spirit of God "blows where it wills," implying that it doesn't always follow predictable patterns or respect our socially constructed boundaries. The wind of the Spirit at Pentecost prompted the disciples to cross language barriers and reach out to people from many lands.[8] Christian movements of renewal

---

[6] Richard Rohr, "Daily Meditation," *Center for Action and Contemplation*, February 6, 2021, https://cac.org/daily-meditations/unknowing-weekly-summary-and-yhwh-prayer-practice-2021-02-06/. I am grateful to my dear friend and colleague Ellen White for introducing me to this bit of wisdom from Rohr.

[7] "Yahweh – Richard Rohr," YouTube video, April 6, 2017, https://www.youtube.com/watch?v=SilgjFpdtwM.

[8] Acts 2:5–12.

and liberation have always looked to the Spirit as a breath of fresh air that calls the church out of self-focused stagnation. The Breath of God blows us toward new ways of expressing God's transformative love in the world.

Since the beginning of human history, breath has signified the spiritual forces of life, creativity, and transformation. As a link to the very Spirit of God, our breath can keep us rooted even as it inspires us to grow. It reminds us of our vitality and gives us courage to face new challenges. It also offers the comfort of knowing we are not alone. Each breath is evidence of God's life-giving Spirit at work around and within us.

Why Try Breath Prayer?

Deep breathing is one of the most efficient techniques for calming the mind and body. The natural rhythm of inhalation and exhalation is soothing. It anchors our often tumultuous thoughts. We rely on breath to sustain our life in each moment, but we rarely notice it happening. Conscious awareness of our breath keeps our mind rooted in the physical reality of the body. This mind-body connection makes Breath Prayer a powerful tool for managing difficult emotions, reducing anxiety, improving sleep, and even boosting creativity.

Our breath is tied directly to our nervous system. When our emotions escalate, our breath gets faster and shallower as part of the *fight/flight/freeze* response. When we relax, it slows down as our bodies go into *rest/digest* mode. This is mostly an involuntary response, but we also have conscious control over our breath. We can choose to slow it down and breathe more deeply. This in turn signals to the rest of our body that it's OK to rest. Our breath is a bit like a thermostat that helps us recognize when our emotional system is amping up then allows us to adjust the dials and regulate ourselves accordingly.

Have you ever watched an athlete just before they start a major competition or a performer just about to go onstage? Almost all of them pause and take a deep breath. They've learned to ground themselves in their bodies to combat the inevitable jitters. It's something I do before preaching and teaching engagements that trigger my fear of public speaking. When anxiety threatens to carry me away, Breath Prayer pulls me back to awareness.

The physiological impact of breathing makes Breath Prayer a great addition to morning or evening routines. Starting each day with a pause to ground ourselves in God's presence can bring clarity for the day ahead. At night, when our minds are spinning with all the events of the day or the worries about tomorrow, focusing on our breath can help settle us for sleep. Whenever I find myself awake in the middle of the night, I've learned to start noticing my breath. The sensations of air flowing in and out of my lungs help block out ruminating thoughts, while breathing slowly and deeply helps my body relax. Awareness of God adds a spiritual element to this natural calming response, enabling me to entrust my concerns to a higher power and focus on the support I receive with each breath.

The simple act of breathing can be a powerful tool for combatting fear. Trauma research has highlighted the value of grounding practices for managing flashbacks and anxiety.[9] Anything that helps us stay present in our bodies and notice physical sensations can bring us back to reality when our minds start to panic. Tying this physical grounding to prayer reminds us we are always connected to a source of support and protection. With Breath Prayer we remind both our bodies and our spirits that right now, in this moment, we are safe and loved.

The phrase "taking a breath" is nearly synonymous with pausing before we respond. Our emotional reactions to the stresses of life can lead to impulsiveness. Our thoughtless responses in the heat of the moment don't always serve us well in the long run. When we stop to notice our breath, it allows us to see ourselves and our situations more clearly. A brief pause gives us a chance to regain control and express ourselves more calmly and effectively. Staying grounded with a short Breath Prayer can also help us feel connected and find more compassion for others.

Pausing to pray with your breath can bring a new perspective in challenging situations. The word *inspiration* literally means "breathing in," so as we inhale we are tapping into God's creative Spirit. As we pause to feel our breath and acknowledge God's presence, we take a step back from our automatic responses to stress. This brief moment can be enough to help us see other options for how to respond. Just as each inhale brings fresh oxygen to fuel our bodies, each Breath Prayer gives us new inspiration for facing our current challenges.

---

[9] Emma Seppälä, et al., "Breathing Based Meditation Decreases Posttraumatic Stress Disorder Symptoms in US Military Veterans: A Randomized Controlled Longitudinal Study," *Journal of Traumatic Stress* 27, no. 4 (2014): 397–405.

Breath Prayer is a fully embodied spiritual practice. We can nourish our bodies, focus our minds, and ground our spirits in the deep awareness of God's Spirit. This holistic experience makes breathing an immensely flexible and effective tool for prayer. With each inhalation we can fill ourselves with the support and love of God. With each exhalation we can release our anxieties into God's hands. Breath Prayer gives us a firm anchor amid the storms that trouble our lives.

How to Practice Breath Prayer

Breath Prayer can be done anywhere or anytime. All you need is your breath! At first it may be helpful to practice in a calm, quiet space to become familiar with the idea of praying with your breath, but feel free to try it out in a variety of settings. The steps are fairly simple:

1) Turn your attention to your breath.

Start by noticing your breath without any pressure to change it. Become more aware of the physical sensations of the air moving in and out or your chest rising and falling. Without any judgment, observe the qualities of your breath (e.g., warm/cool, fast/slow, deep/shallow).

2) Breathe in.

Each time you inhale, imagine yourself breathing in God's Spirit. Let your body and mind fill up with the love and grace of God. If you find it helpful, select a word or phrase to repeat silently with your inhalation, such as "I breathe in God's grace."

3) Breathe out.

Each time you exhale, imagine yourself breathing that same compassionate Spirit out into the world. Picture the space around you filling up with God's love. Again, feel free to use a word or phrase such as "I breathe out God's peace." If there is a particular worry or concern that you'd like to offer up to God, imagine it physically flowing out of you as you exhale.

4) Continue breathing.

Repeat your phrases or simply notice each time you inhale and exhale. Keep your mind focused on your breath and the Presence of God nourishing you in this moment.

Tips for Practicing Breath Prayer

Don't overthink it. Breath Prayer really is as simple as breathing in and out. If adding words or images helps you focus, great! If not, skip that part and just focus on the physical sensation of breathing. Trust that God is present in each breath.

Build it into your routine. Practice your Breath Prayer first thing in the morning to focus for the day, or try it at bedtime to reconnect with God and let go of the day's stresses.

Set an alarm. Use your phone or watch to remind you to try Breath Prayer at random times of day. Whenever the alarm goes off, take a few moments to breathe and pray in the midst of whatever you're doing.

Reflection

Once you've had a chance to try Breath Prayer a few times, take a moment to reflect using the questions below. You can journal your responses, talk to a friend or spiritual director, or think through the questions silently.

- What was your experience practicing Breath Prayer?
- What made it easier or more difficult?
- Where in your body did you most notice your breath?
- How did you experience God's presence during Breath Prayer?
- In what situations do you think Breath Prayer will especially benefit you?

CHAPTER 7

Activation: Pilgrimage

I am about to do a new thing; now it springs forth; do you not perceive it? I will make a way in the wilderness and rivers in the desert. —Isaiah 43:19

Feeling stuck is one of the most frustrating human experiences. Whether we're sitting in a traffic jam or feeling stagnant in our career, a sense of restlessness grows in us. It's the same reason many people feel claustrophobic in elevators: we're hardwired to want a way out. We crave movement and progress, both physically and in our personal and spiritual lives.

Many aspects of our culture contribute to feelings of stagnation. With the technology to access everything we need at the tap of a touchscreen, we spend an increasing portion of our waking hours doing sedentary activities. We don't even need to leave the house for groceries because we can have them delivered to our doorsteps. Our engagement with social media can also leave us feeling stuck as we compare our real and often frustrating daily lives to the carefully curated images of influencers.

Movement is the natural antidote to feeling stuck. It's the opposite of stagnation and passivity. The concept of "activation" involves making ourselves more active. Getting ourselves moving and changing our scenery can shift our perspective. It opens new possibilities for growth and creativity. When we're stuck on a problem, it's common advice to step away for a while and come back to the situation fresh. The same logic can apply to our spiritual lives. If we're feeling stagnant in our faith, it can help to get moving and change our vantage point. Spiritual activation can be a practice of seeking God's presence in new places and activities. Instead of passively waiting for God to show up, we take an active role.

The rich tradition of pilgrimage provides a template for activation in our spiritual lives. People of faith have been making sacred journeys since the earliest stories of scripture, but many of us have lost touch with that practice. We associate pilgrimage with long-distance travel and write it off as too expensive and time-consuming. But, in fact, any movement we engage with spiritual intention can be a pilgrimage. We can reconnect with God's active presence in our lives by getting ourselves moving in new ways.

What Is Pilgrimage?

Pilgrimage captures the essence of spiritual activation by linking movement to a sacred goal. *A pilgrimage is an active journey toward something holy.* The destination can be a particular sacred site or a broader spiritual goal such as compassion or peace. We travel toward that goal with our whole selves. We move our bodies in order to refresh our souls.

Traditionally pilgrimage has taken the form of geographical travel. Pilgrims often leave familiar places in search of new experiences of God. They visit locations that hold spiritual significance, such as the site of a miraculous event or the burial place of a holy person. They have a destination in mind, but along the way they often find transformation in the journey itself.

Traveling is a common form of pilgrimage, but it's certainly not the only option. A simple walk, roll, or ride with prayerful attention to God's presence can be a pilgrimage. So can tracing a finger labyrinth or visiting someone in need. A pilgrim can stay close to home, but step outside their usual routines. We might seek out a breathtaking landscape or immerse ourselves in a different culture to experience God in a new way. Any form of movement that brings us to a new vantage point can help expand our awareness of God's presence in the world.

Pilgrimage leads us outside our comfort zone. Leaving familiar places and routines can feel awkward, but that strangeness sparks new insight.[1] When we place ourselves in a new environment, we see things differently. We encounter God in new places and people. By experiencing the vulnerability of being an outsider, we increase our

---

[1] Christine Valters Paintner has a chapter titled "The Practice of Being Uncomfortable" in her wonderful book *The Soul of a Pilgrim: Eight Practices for the Journey Within* (Notre Dame, IN: Sorin Books, 2015).

capacity for compassion. Pilgrimage reminds us to look beyond our own perspective and connect with others.

Pilgrimage as a practice of spiritual activation can be linked to activism. It's not a coincidence that the words "activation" and "activism" have the same root. Both imply movement and agency. Activism becomes a spiritual practice when it's rooted in God's call for social righteousness. Clergy friends of mine who were active in the 2014 demonstrations in Ferguson, Missouri, held signs saying, "We're praying with our feet." This phrase, first used by Frederick Douglass,[2] is an apt description of Pilgrimage. Protest marches and demonstrations are pilgrimages toward the holy vision of a more just and loving world.[3]

After a pilgrimage, we return home. We bring our fresh insights back to help reshape our lives. The pilgrimage experience sheds new light on our familiar places and habits. We may find deeper appreciation for things we once took for granted, or we might reevaluate our priorities and make changes accordingly. The understanding gained in new places needs to be integrated into our old ways of seeing the world.

Wherever pilgrimage takes us, we return changed. It may not be a dramatic movement, but each new experience shifts our perspective. By seeking out the unfamiliar, we invite God's Spirit to guide us out of our stagnation. As we step outside our usual routines, we expand our understanding of God and of ourselves. We become active partners in the work God is doing in the world.

Pilgrimage in Scripture and Tradition

Movement has long been an element of faith. Abraham and Sarah left their home to follow God's call.[4] The Israelites journeyed from Egypt to the promised land.[5] Jesus and his disciples traveled from Galilee to Jerusalem before his death.[6] Paul traversed the Roman

---

[2] Both Frederick Douglass in accounts of his personal journey to freedom and Abraham Joshua Heschel in his description of his participation in the 1965 Selma marches used the phrase. Both are quoted variously. For a brief summary, see Justice Baird, "Praying with my Feet," *Sefaria*, accessed August 31, 2024, https://www.sefaria.org/sheets/25820?lang=bi.

[3] Barbara Holmes uses this imagery to describe the Civil Rights marches of the 1960s: "I find that the spiritual destination of these justice processions was the consciousness of the nation." *Joy Unspeakable*, 116.

[4] Genesis 12:1–9.

[5] The whole book of Exodus recounts this journey.

[6] Jesus' journey to Jerusalem is told in all four Gospels. See, for example, Matthew 20:17–18; Mark 10:32; Luke 13:22, 19:28; and John 11:7.

Empire to spread the gospel message.[7] The Bible is full of people engaging with God as they move from place to place.

The practice of pilgrimage developed as new generations of Christians began traveling to sacred places in search of deeper connection to God. Holy relics, burial places of saints, and sites of reported divine visitation all drew pilgrims hoping to experience something transcendent. The famous Camino de Santiago in Spain is still an active pilgrimage route that draws both spiritual and secular travelers. Many Christians also consider travel to Israel/Palestine a pilgrimage to walk the land Jesus walked.

The metaphor of a "faith journey" takes its root from all these stories of physical journeying. Symbolic representations of pilgrimage such as John Bunyan's *Pilgrim's Progress* promoted the idea that the life of faith is a progressive movement toward God. Medieval cathedrals developed prayer labyrinths as a symbolic pilgrimage for those who couldn't travel physically. Labyrinths represent spiritual movement through the visual shape of a maze that has no wrong turns. There is only one winding path to the center. The goal of a labyrinth is not to solve the maze but simply to follow the path. These traditions shifted the focus of pilgrimage away from long-distance travel and toward an interior journey of personal transformation.

Faith-based movements for social change have also used the language of pilgrimage. Dorothy Day, a leader of the Catholic Worker movement in the mid-twentieth century, wrote a regular column titled "On Pilgrimage," in which she reflected on her day-to-day experiences living out her faith among the underprivileged. As her friend and editor, Jim Forrest, wrote, "Pilgrimage for Dorothy was a way of life, a mode of listening, an attitude that motivated choices, a discipline of being."[8] The American Civil Rights Movement likewise consciously adopted language of pilgrimage to express the journey toward freedom and equality.[9]

---

[7] Acts 13–21, 27–28.

[8] Jim Forrest, quoted in Dorothy Day, *On Pilgrimage: The Sixties: A Chronicle of Faith and Action through a Decade of Protest, Idealism, and Change*, ed. Robert Ellsberg (Maryknoll, NY: Orbis Books, 2021), xvii.

[9] For example, a 1957 demonstration in Washington, D.C., was named "The Prayer Pilgrimage for Freedom." The Martin Luther King Jr. Research and Education Institute, Stanford University, accessed August 19, 2024, https://kinginstitute.stanford.edu/prayer-pilgrimage-freedom#:~:text=On%20 17%20May%201957%2C%20nearly%2025%2C000%20demonstrators%20 gathered,the%20three-year-old%20Brown%20v.%20Board%20of%20 Education%20decision.

Theological reflections on social justice movements have highlighted the role of activation in embodying the teachings of Scripture. They emphasize the importance of "praxis," or lived practice as a counterbalance to abstract theological reflection. Known as liberation theologies, these movements took seriously the biblical accounts of God freeing people from bondage and establishing new social orders.[10] The Exodus from Egypt became a metaphor for the pilgrimage toward justice in modern society.

Even in contemporary secular culture we find recognition of pilgrimage as a tool for spiritual awakening. Popular novels-turned-films like *Wild* and *Eat, Pray, Love* feature women going on journeys to find a new sense of meaning at crucial junctures in life. The 2010 film *The Way* is set on the actual pilgrimage path of the Camino de Santiago. It portrays a father's search for closure after his son's death, leading him to a broader personal awakening. These films highlight the role of traveling outside one's comfort zone to find new insight.

Christian tradition has never been sedentary. The faith itself spread from its geographical roots in a small Middle Eastern territory to reach people around the globe. For centuries people have sought active ways to engage their beliefs and deepen their spirituality. People have responded to God's call to action by traveling to new places or embarking on new experiences. People of faith have always journeyed in search of fresh experiences of God.

Why Try Pilgrimage?

Pilgrimage provides both physical and spiritual activation. It literally gets us moving. We step out of our sedentary routines and into new experiences of God and the world. This movement has benefits for our physical, mental, and emotional health. It can help us get unstuck, both internally and externally. Thomas Merton discussed the value of both the external and internal journeys of pilgrimage, saying: "One can have one without the other. It is best to have both."[11]

Therapists often recommend something called "behavioral activation" for people experiencing depression. It entails getting up and doing things that generate positive emotions, even if the activities

---

[10] See the book of Exodus; Matthew 21:12; Luke 4:18; Acts 4;32; James 1:9–10; etc.

[11] Thomas Merton, *Mystics and Zen Masters* (New York: Farrar, Straus and Giroux, 1967), 33.

don't sound appealing at first.[12] Physical exercise can be a part of this activation, but it also includes activities that provide a sense of meaning and purpose. Positive emotions are generated by activities that align with our values and goals. Spiritual pilgrimage combines both the physical and value-based aspects of behavioral activation. By engaging in movement with a meaningful goal, we can start to shift our emotional perspective.

Most of us know movement is good for us. We hear it from our doctors, magazines, and advertisers claiming their products will magically make us want to exercise. Exercise can improve our mood, reduce the effects of stress, and increase blood flow to our brains.[13] The problem is that exercise for its own sake often feels tedious and boring. Having a particular goal or destination makes movement feel more purposeful. Spiritual activation keeps our focus on connection with God rather than how many steps we've taken or how many calories we've burned. A regular practice of pilgrimage can help us develop an active lifestyle that feels more meaningful.

New experiences and physical movement are both tied to increased creativity. Pilgrimage forces us to get out of old ruts and explore new ways of being. Our brains tend to create default patterns based on our familiar routines.[14] The stimulation of a new environment helps our minds build new pathways and connections. Research studies have linked exposure to novel experiences with the ability to generate new ideas.[15] They have also shown physical movement to enhance creativity by increasing blood flow and plasticity in the brain.[16] The movement

---

[12] For an overview of behavioral activation, see Zawn Villines, "What is Behavioral Activation?" *Medical News Today*, October 25, 2021, https://www.medicalnewstoday.com/articles/behavioral-activation, accessed 8/5/24.

[13] See Arlene Semeco, "The Top 10 Benefits of Regular Exercise," *Healthline*, November 13, 2023, https://www.healthline.com/nutrition/10-benefits-of-exercise.

[14] Norman Fab, a Canadian neuroscientist and psychologist, discusses this concept of the "default mode network" in an episode of the *Hidden Brain* podcast with Shankar Vedatantam. "Changing Our Mental Maps," *Hidden Brain*, 2024, transcription: https://app.podscribe.ai/episode/106134136.

[15] "Why Opening Up to New Experiences Can Get the Creative Juices Flowing," University of Bath, July 31, 2018, last modified January 15, 2019, https://www.bath.ac.uk/announcements/why-opening-up-to-new-experiences-can-get-the-creative-juices-flowing/.

[16] Nikolas J. Stimpson, Glen Davison, and Amir-Homayoun Javadi, "Joggin' the Noggin: Towards a Physiological Understanding of Exercise-Induced Cognitive Benefits," *Neuroscience & Biobehavioral Reviews* 88 (2018): 177–186, https://doi.org/10.1016/j.neubiorev.2018.03.018.

and novelty need not be extreme to reap these benefits. Any pilgrimage that gets us active in new ways can be a source of inspiration.

The outward focus of pilgrimage can also help shift our thinking patterns. Anxiety naturally pulls us into a self-protective mindset. We become caught in vicious cycles of "what if?" thoughts that keep us from acting. Pilgrimage forces us to break out of that pattern physically and mentally. Experiencing new places reminds us that the world is larger than our daily worries. Meeting new people draws us out of ourselves and enhances our capacity for connection and compassion. Actively engaging in the new things God is doing around us can combat our anxious ruminations.

In the summer of 2020, at the height of the global COVID-19 pandemic, a friend and colleague of mine went on a pilgrimage. Despite being an immunocompromised black man, he felt called to respond to the increasing fear and unrest across the United States by walking across the country, coast to coast. His hundred-day trek embodied the shift from anxious stagnation to active connection. Instead of staying safely at home in a time of real danger, my friend left his familiar routines to encounter new places and people. His journey did not always go as expected, but he found friendship and inspiration at every turn. We may not all be called to such a bold journey, but we too can activate our spiritual development through the practice of pilgrimage.

How to Practice Pilgrimage

Your pilgrimage need not be an elaborate journey. The goal is to move your body in some way toward a sacred intention. Whether you visit a new place, stroll or roll around your neighborhood, or take action toward a meaningful goal, focus on how the experience reveals God to you in new ways.

A few options for pilgrimage include:

- *Prayer Walk, Roll, or Ride:* Set a destination in your neighborhood or along a favorite trail. Invite God to help you experience the journey with fresh eyes and an open heart.

- *Prayer Labyrinth:* Find a church or retreat center with an outdoor labyrinth, or print out an image of a finger labyrinth. Trace the path slowly and prayerfully until you reach the center, reflecting on your own spiritual journey.

- *Cultural Engagement:* Challenge yourself to experience something outside your comfort zone. Visit an unfamiliar church service or cultural event.

- *Social Action:* Do something concrete to enact your spiritual beliefs and values. Participate in a demonstration or volunteer for a charity.

The following steps can be adapted to any variation, including your own creative version of a pilgrimage.

1) Identify your destination.

If you intend to travel somewhere physically, be clear why you have selected this place and what spiritual significance it holds for you. If your destination is more abstract, put the goal into words, for example: "I am tracing this labyrinth to seek God's guidance," or "I will volunteer at the soup kitchen to live out my commitment to help others."

2) Begin with prayer.

Take a moment at the start of your journey to invite God to travel with you. This can be a verbal prayer or simply a moment of silence before you embark. Ask God to help you remain open throughout the experience.

3) Stay present to the journey.

Distractions are inevitable, but do your best to stay attentive throughout your pilgrimage. Observe your surroundings in detail. Notice the physical sensations of movement as well as any thoughts and emotions that arise in you.

4) Expect the unexpected.

Allow the journey to evolve as you go. You have a destination in mind, but the path may wander. Let yourself turn down an unfamiliar road or explore new questions that arise. Even the destination itself may turn out differently than you imagined.

5) Return home with gratitude.

Thank God for the experience of your pilgrimage. Note any insights or perspectives you have gained from the journey. Consider how you might integrate these new understandings as you return to familiar routines.

Tips for Practicing Pilgrimage

Don't rush. Move at a comfortable pace, respecting your physical, mental, and emotional energy levels. Pilgrimage is not a race and there is no time limit. Allow yourself time to rest.

Keep an open mind. Pilgrimage is about experiencing something new. Try to let go of any judgments that arise. Focus on taking in the experience just as it is.

Embrace discomfort. Pilgrimage is not always going to be pleasant. Invite yourself to sit with your discomfort and welcome any insights that arise from it.

Seek connection. Notice the ways this new experience connects you to others, to God, and to the world around you. Instead of focusing on what's different in an unfamiliar setting, observe the commonalities.

Reflection

Once you've had a chance to try pilgrimage a few times, take a moment to reflect using the questions below. You can journal your responses, talk to a friend or spiritual director, or think through them silently.

- What destination did you choose, and why?
- What emotions came up during the journey?
- In what ways did you encounter God?
- What new insights did you find along the way?
- In what ways has your perspective changed?

CHAPTER 8

Gratitude: Prayerful Savoring

Taste and see that the Lord is good.   —Psalm 34:8

The hectic pace of our lives makes it easy to overlook moments of simple joy. We rush through our meals without really tasting them. We hurry along our daily commutes and don't notice the beautiful way the sun reflects off the clouds. We're so busy working through our to-do lists that we don't hear the birds singing. We rarely stop to smell the roses, literally or figuratively, so we miss out on these opportunities for everyday enjoyment.

We human beings are sensory creatures. God gave us sight, sound, taste, touch, and smell to explore and appreciate the world around us. When we slow down and pay attention to everything our senses take in, we often find a sense of awe and gratitude. We are surrounded by beauty and wonder. Engaging our full sensory experience can help us savor the goodness of what God has made.

Sensory pleasure is at the heart of many of the celebrations in our lives. We play music at parties and eat good food on holidays. We decorate our spaces or seek beautiful venues for significant events. We light candles and burn incense. We dance to feel our bodies moving. Our expressions of joy and festivity are instinctively embodied. We use our senses to increase our enjoyment and gratitude in these moments.

As a spiritual practice, gratitude helps us focus on what's good in our lives. It's easy to get bogged down with worries and complaints. There's a lot about our world we'd like to change, but appreciating moments of joy when they arise can give us the energy and hope we need to keep working toward our goals. A regular practice of Prayerful Savoring can fill us up with these experiences of simple pleasure and help us feel grateful for what God has given us.

What Is Prayerful Savoring?

Prayerful Savoring is the intentional practice of enjoying our physical senses. It's a practice of gratitude for the beauty of what we can see, hear, taste, smell, and touch. Instead of focusing on the flaws and defects of our experience, we seek out and acknowledge what is good. The word *savoring* implies lingering in these pleasant sensations. We not only notice what's good; we relish it. We dwell on it. We choose not to rush on to the next task because we want to fully absorb the richness of our current experience. When I put a piece of good dark chocolate on my tongue, I don't rush to chew and swallow it. I let it melt slowly. It's my favorite way to tune out the world and enjoy a moment of pleasure.

There's something celebratory about savoring. It feels like a special treat to eat that piece of chocolate or enjoy a few extra minutes in a nice hot shower. Many of our daily experiences don't inspire savoring. Taking out the trash, for example, is not exactly a pleasant sensory experience. The contrast between these mundane activities and the moments we choose to savor can enhance the feeling of gratitude. *Prayerful Savoring is an act of celebrating the shimmering moments of pleasure that stand out amid our daily grind.*

Savoring requires us to engage in moments of joy as they arise. Many popular gratitude practices, such as journaling, work retroactively. You look back at the day or week and try to remember good things that happened.[1] There's evidence that this trains our mind to notice more good things in the future, but it doesn't provide a means for expressing gratitude in real time. Prayerful Savoring focuses on the moment of joy itself as an act of prayer. By attending to pleasant sensations and fully experiencing them with gratitude, we can acknowledge the gifts God gives us in the very moment we receive them.

Practicing gratitude does not negate our experiences of suffering. It's not the sort of "toxic positivity" that prioritizes optimism at the expense of healthy emotional expression. There is plenty of room in our spiritual lives for expressions of sadness, anger, and guilt. Just look at the book of Psalms! Prayerful Savoring is not a tool for blocking

---

[1] The Greater Good Science Center at UC Berkeley suggests a practice it calls "Three Good Things." This practice entails writing a detailed account of three things that went well every day. You can check out the practice and the research behind it here: https://ggia.berkeley.edu/practice/three-good-things (accessed August 10, 2024).

out these emotions, but rather an invitation to acknowledge the good alongside the painful experiences.[2]

We can prayerfully savor just about any pleasant experience by tuning in to our senses. Taking that first slow sip of hot coffee in the morning can be a prayer. Feeling the sun on our skin on the first warm day of spring is an experience of grace. Listening to a favorite song with our full attention (instead of using it as background noise) helps us fully appreciate the gift of music. When we stop to admire a delicate flower or appreciate the damp, earthy smell after a rainstorm, we have an opportunity to share our moment of joy with God. Prayerful Savoring helps us bring gratitude into these daily moments and reminds us that all good things come from God.

Gratitude is related to our sense of awe. Children naturally express wonder at the world around them. When I take my son and daughter for a walk around the neighborhood, they pick up rocks like treasures. They notice every birdcall and point out each tiny plant sprouting in the cracks of the sidewalk. Their senses are always open, and they take nothing for granted. Prayerful Savoring is an invitation to reawaken that childlike curiosity in all of us.[3] We can explore the world as if for the first time, letting our experiences renew our appreciation for the wonder of creation.

Prayerful Savoring in Scripture and Tradition

There's a refrain throughout the creation story in the first chapter of Genesis: "God saw that it was good."[4] After each step in the process of forming the universe, God stopped to admire the beauty of it all. And in that same story we learn that humankind was created in the very image of God.[5] One way we can reflect that image is by joining God in appreciating the glorious world God created. Savoring beauty in its many forms connects us to God, who acknowledged the goodness of each piece of creation.

---

[2] If you struggle to find any moments of joy or gratitude over the course of a week or more, please reach out to a mental health professional as this can be a sign of more serious mental health concerns.

[3] Zen Buddhist tradition teaches a similar concept, known as "beginner's mind." The focus of that teaching is on staying open-minded and letting go of preconceived ideas about our experiences. Prayerful Savoring differs in its emphasis on gratitude and enjoyment.

[4] Genesis 1:4, 10, 12, 18, 21, 25, 31.

[5] Genesis 1:27.

The Psalms offer numerous examples of gratitude for the wonder of creation. Psalm 104 paints a multi-sensory picture of God's amazing works: God stretching out the heavens like a tent, thundering commands at the mountains and seas, watering the trees, and feeding the animals. God's hand and God's breath provide tangible sources of life, inspiring the psalmist to sing praise for it all. Psalm 8 likewise marvels at the role of humanity in contrast to the vast heavens: "What are humans that you are mindful them, mortals that you care for them?" (v. 4). This theme of awe and gratitude for everything God created recurs throughout the book of Psalms.[6]

In the Sermon on the Mount, Jesus points to the beauty of creation as an antidote for worry.[7] Look at the birds, he says. They enjoy the food God provides without stockpiling for the future. Consider the wildflowers. Their beauty is incomparable even though they last only a few days. I don't think Jesus is being naïve about our basic needs. He's reminding us that our fears and concerns aren't the whole picture. Looking to the natural world reminds us of all the good things God already provides. Jesus highlights the value of gratitude for keeping anxiety in check.

Later, when Jesus sits down for his last supper with the disciples, he gives thanks for the bread and wine.[8] This basic meal blessing was a standard part of Jewish culture at the time,[9] but it took on new meaning for Christians when Jesus tied it to his death and resurrection. The aspect of gratitude was so important to early Christians that they named the sacrament of the Lord's Supper *eucharist*, which is Greek for "thanksgiving." Every time Christians celebrate communion, it is an act of thanksgiving expressed through the sensory experiences of eating and drinking.

During the Middle Ages, Christian mystics often used sensory imagery to describe their encounters with God.[10] Some, like Bernard of Clairvaux, looked to the biblical Song of Songs as a sensual

---

[6] See Psalms 19, 33, 65, 98, 147, etc.

[7] Matthew 6:25–31.

[8] Matthew 26:26–28; Mark 14:22–24; Luke 22:19–20; and 1 Corinthians 11:23–29.

[9] For more on Jewish meal blessings, see "Blessings for Food & Drink," My Jewish Learning, accessed August 9, 2024, https://www.myjewishlearning.com/article/blessings-for-food-drink/.

[10] Patricia Dailey, "The Body and Its Senses" in *The Cambridge Companion to Christian Mysticism*, ed. Amy Hollywood and Patricia Z. Beckman (Cambridge, UK: Cambridge University Press, 2012), 264–76.

metaphor for the soul's relationship to God. Others, like Mechthild of Magdeburg, describe "eating God" and tasting the Word in their mouths. Hildegard of Bingen is famous for her musical compositions, many of which include luscious descriptions of the beauty of creation. These spiritual writers recognized that their physical senses were an avenue for connection with the goodness of God.

The influence of dualistic thinking on Eurocentric Christianity has led to a distrust (and even vilification) of sensory enjoyment. In contrast, other cultural expressions of faith celebrate and worship in fully embodied ways. Barbara Holmes highlights the role of song and dance in African American spirituality as an expression of the "Joy Unspeakable" that defines encounter with God.[11] Holmes notes that the word "rejoice" in the Aramaic dialect of Jesus can also be translated "dance."[12] This gives a whole new vision to verses such as Luke 6:23a: "Dance on that day and leap for joy, for surely your reward is great in heaven."[13] Authentic expression of gratitude has long involved celebratory movement.

American Christians often associate gratitude with the Thanksgiving holiday. Despite the colonialist roots of this celebration, there is something profound about having a designated holiday for the purpose of giving thanks. It is one of the few times our consumerist culture prioritizes gratitude, and it's characterized by a sensory feast. We gather around the table with loved ones, appreciating the gift of community, and we enjoy the delights of our senses together. The smells of turkey roasting, the texture of perfectly mashed potatoes, and the savory taste of stuffing are meant to evoke gratitude for the bounty of our lives. The ongoing popularity of Thanksgiving traditions speaks to our cultural hunger for sensory expressions of gratitude.

Why Try Prayerful Savoring?

As human beings we have an innate "negativity bias."[14] We're more attentive to negative events because our brains perceive them as problems to be solved. When good things happen there's nothing

---

[11] Barbara Holmes, *Joy Unspeakable: Contemplative Practices of the Black Church* (Minneapolis, MI: Fortress, 2017).

[12] Holmes, *Joy Unspeakable*, 76.

[13] Other verses where you might imagine dancing include Luke 10:21, 15:6, 15:32; Matthew 5:12; and John 3:29, 5:35, 20:20.

[14] This is a well-documented psychological phenomenon. See, for example: https://positivepsychology.com/3-steps-negativity-bias/ (accessed June 11, 2024).

to solve, so our brains don't prioritize them. As a result, we spend a lot more time thinking about what goes wrong than what goes right. I notice it most in how I process feedback from others. If I get nine compliments and only one criticism, I'm going to brood over that single criticism. Ruminating on our negative experiences can leave us feeling disheartened, but gratitude can tip the balance back toward what's going well in our lives.

When we focus on what we're thankful for, we spend less time in a state of stress. Reducing stress is tied to many other aspects of well-being. Studies have shown direct links between gratitude and cardiac health.[15] Feeling awe has been shown to activate the vagal nerves, promoting deeper breathing and slower heartrate.[16] A paper titled "The Science of Gratitude," published by the Greater Good Science Center, lists numerous benefits including better physical and mental health, increased happiness, stronger relationships, and even increased productivity.[17] Shifting our attention toward gratitude can free up the energy we would otherwise spend worrying and stewing.

Much of the research talks about gratitude in the abstract. There's little attention given to the relational nature of giving thanks. When a friend gives me a gift, my thanks are directed to that person. When I notice a beautiful sunset, my gratitude also has a direction. Acknowledging how God created all the pleasant things I experience adds an element of connection to my gratitude practice. It's like the difference between noticing a piece of artwork you enjoy then getting the chance to meet the artist and share your appreciation directly. Gratitude becomes a spiritual practice when it brings us into deeper relationship with God as we enjoy what God created.

Professor of Aesthetics Elaine Scarry argues there is a direct link between appreciation of beauty and acknowledgment of justice.[18] She highlights the way in which beauty catches us off guard and causes

[15] Paul J. Mills, Laura Redwine, and Deepak Chopra, "A Grateful Heart May Be a Healthier Heart," *Spirituality in Clinical Practice* 2, no. 1 (2015): 23–24, doi:10.1037/scp0000063.

[16] Hope Rease, "How a Bit of Awe Can Improve Your Health," *The New York Times*, January 3, 2023, https://www.nytimes.com/2023/01/03/well/live/awe-wonder-dacher-keltner.html.

[17] Greater Good Science Center, *The Science of Gratitude*, May 2018, https://ggsc.berkeley.edu/images/uploads/GGSC-JTF_White_Paper-Gratitude-FINAL.pdf.

[18] Elaine Scarry, *On Beauty and Being Just* (Princeton, NJ: Princeton University Press, 1999).

us to "decenter" ourselves. Those moments when we stand in awe of something remind us that the world is much bigger than our limited perspective. Such moments of beauty and goodness are longed for and deserved by all people. Our gratitude for personal experiences can spur us to create more beauty, goodness, and justice in the world.

Gratitude is also closely linked with generosity. Those who appreciate what they have are much more likely to share it with others. Scientists have used brain imaging to identify that expressions of gratitude and generosity occur via the same neural networks. They also observed that practicing gratitude increases the sense of pleasure people feel when making charitable gifts.[19] Gratitude reminds us of all the ways we benefit from the community around us. This in turn motivates us to make our own contributions by sharing what we can.

The practice of Prayerful Savoring helps shift our focus from our natural proclivity for negativity toward an appreciation of the ways God is blessing us each day. It doesn't erase our suffering, but it broadens our awareness to include the everyday pleasures that our senses can provide. By taking note of the positive experiences and intentionally savoring them, we fill up our stores of joy and gratitude. Gratitude gives us fuel to face the difficulties of life and extend goodness to those around us.

How to Practice Prayerful Savoring

Prayerful Savoring can be done with just about any sensory experience: the taste of food, the sound of music, the sight of a work of art. You could try savoring a good hug with a loved one or soaking in a warm bath. Essential oils or scented candles are great tools for this practice as well. My favorite Prayerful Savoring activity is going for a nature walk and letting all my senses explore the beauty of God's creation. Be creative, and let your sense of enjoyment be your guide.

1) Notice something good.

It's hard to savor something if you don't realize it's happening. Prayerful Savoring starts with opening ourselves to the world around us and noticing the good things that are there. Try bringing new awareness to some of your daily activities, and see what good there is to notice.

---

[19] Sigal Samuel, "Giving Thanks May Make Your Brain More Altruistic," *Vox*, November 24, 2020, https://www.vox.com/future-perfect/2019/11/27/20983850/gratitude-altruism-charity-generosity-neuroscience.

2) Explore it with your senses.

Allow yourself to experience this good thing with as many of your senses as possible. What can you see? Hear? Smell? Taste? Feel? Let yourself be curious and explore as if you've never had this experience before.

3) Express gratitude.

Take note of what you appreciate in this moment. You can use words, but you don't have to. A smile, a laugh, or a sigh can tell God how thankful you are for whatever you're experiencing. Let your gratitude arise naturally; there's no need to force it. Feeling like you "should" be grateful is not really savoring.

4) Linger in the enjoyment.

Our minds are prone to wander, so it may take practice to stay fully engaged in Prayerful Savoring. Whenever you notice other thoughts come to your mind, return to the awareness of your senses and let that help you stay in the moment. Try not to rush this experience; let yourself stay and enjoy it for a while!

Tips for Practicing Prayerful Savoring

Start small. Pick one enjoyable thing you do every day—drinking your morning coffee or listening to your favorite playlist. Commit to focusing all your attention on it, and fully appreciate the moment of joy.

Express yourself. Use art, music, or poetry as a creative outlet for the gratitude that arises from your Prayerful Savoring practice.

Pick one sense each day. Focusing on one sense at a time can help structure your practice. For example, take one day to explore your sense of smell. Notice as many pleasurable smells as you can. Then move on to another sense the next day.

Reflection

Once you've had a chance to try Prayerful Savoring a few times, take a moment to reflect using the questions below. You can journal your responses, talk to a friend or spiritual director, or think through them silently.

- What did your Prayerful Savoring experiences have in common?
- Which of your senses were most easily engaged?
- Was it difficult to connect with any particular sense(s)? Which one(s)?
- In what ways did you experience and express gratitude?
- How was God present in your moments of joy?

CHAPTER 9

Intimacy: Soul Friends

As perfume and incense make the heart rejoice, such is the sweetness of a friend's soulful counsel.   —Proverbs 27:9

It's no secret that our culture is increasingly fostering disconnection. Despite all our "social" media, we often find it hard to connect to others in deep, meaningful ways. In 2023 U.S. Surgeon General Vivek Murthy issued a public health advisory entitled "Our Epidemic of Loneliness and Isolation."[1] The advisory sought to raise awareness about the very real mental and physical health impacts of decreased social connection.

Cultural values of individualism and self-sufficiency intensify our isolation. Many of us, especially those raised in white, middle-class communities, grew up learning that depending on others is a sign of weakness. "Do-it-yourself" is not just a home-improvement category; it's a motto for life. Emotional and spiritual struggles are labeled "personal problems" and are accordingly kept private. Social relationships tend to remain superficial. We talk about the weather, our favorite movies, or shared activities. We rarely delve into our deeper thoughts and feelings.

Even faith has been permeated by this individualism. The focus on a "personal relationship" with God often overshadows the communal aspects of faith. Our identity as Christians tends to focus on individual beliefs rather than on our role within the family of God. Not only

---

[1] Office of the U.S. Surgeon General, *Our Epidemic of Loneliness and Isolation: The U.S. Attorney General's Advisory on the Healing Effects of Connection and Community*, 2023, https://www.hhs.gov/sites/default/files/surgeon-general-social-connection-advisory.pdf.

does this stray from the biblical image of the church as the collective body of Christ, but it also opens the door for individualistic morality that evades accountability to others.

These cultural factors prompted me to conclude *Sacred Balance* with an intentionally relational spiritual practice. The Celtic tradition of the "soul friend," or *anam cara*, can be a powerful antidote to loneliness and individualism. It creates a structure for relationship that goes deeper than our usual chitchat. Having a conversation partner committed to exploring our spiritual well-being enables us to build a deeply nourishing sense of intimacy. We can also gain valuable insight from the other person's point of view.

What is a Soul Friend?

Soul Friendship is a conscious commitment to explore with another person the deeper facets of our spiritual lives. As Irish poet and author John O'Donohue describes it, the Soul Friend is "a person to whom you could reveal the hidden intimacies of your life."[2] Soul Friends share their experiences of God, their faith questions, and their hopes for spiritual growth. They may challenge each other to consider new perspectives or hold each other accountable to commitments they have made. A Soul Friend can be a mirror that helps us to see ourselves more clearly. This level of intimacy requires genuineness, honesty, and vulnerability.

The term "intimacy," despite its use as a euphemism for sexual activity, is not exclusive to sexual or even romantic relationships. *Intimacy is the sense of closeness that grows from sharing personal aspects of ourselves with others.* This may include physical intimacy, but it also encompasses the many ways in which we share our thoughts, feelings, and experiences with people in our lives. I think of times when I disclose an embarrassing moment to a close friend or let family members care for me when I'm sick and miserable. I trust these people not to judge me, so letting them see my vulnerable moments feels safe and comforting. Even a shared joke with a coworker can promote a sense of intimacy by revealing my sense of humor and establishing a closer connection. Spiritual intimacy develops when we allow someone to know the joys, fears, desires, and questions that shape our relationship to the Divine.

---

[2] John O'Donohue, *Anam Cara: A Book of Celtic Wisdom* (San Francisco, CA: Harper Collins, 1997), xviii.

A Soul Friend also reminds us our faith is about more than ourselves. We are created for community, and we experience God with and through other people. O'Donohue compares the Soul Friend to the Buddhist tradition of the "noble friend" who kindly confronts our blind spots in order to help us see ourselves more clearly.[3] The honest perspective of a Soul Friend can help protect us from myopic views of God and ourselves. It requires a great deal of trust, not to mention humility, to allow (and even welcome) our spiritual lives to be refined in this way.

An attitude of hospitality characterizes Soul Friendship. In this practice we create space for one another. We welcome each other's thoughts and experiences with grace instead of judgment. Sharing our deep spiritual longings and fears requires vulnerability, so Soul Friends must be prepared to receive that vulnerability with care. Instead of advice giving, Soul Friends focus on listening deeply and sharing observations or questions that arise. Setting clear expectations for the relationship creates the safety needed to be honest about our spiritual lives.

It can be helpful to differentiate Soul Friendship from other types of relationships. Soul Friendship can sometimes develop out of a casual connection, but as a spiritual practice it requires a deeper level of intentionality and trust. A Soul Friend provides more than just pleasant conversation. On the other hand, Soul Friendship is not therapy. It is not intended to address serious psychological issues or emotional distress. Therapy is a professional relationship that requires extensive training and safeguards to protect the client's welfare. Soul Friendship is mutual; it depends on a shared commitment to explore and support each other's spiritual growth. Soul Friends can share insights gained in personal therapy and may help highlight areas where deeper therapeutic work is needed. They should not depend on one another as replacements for a professional therapist.

One particular expression of Soul Friendship is spiritual direction. A spiritual director is a trained guide who helps others discern the work of the Holy Spirit in their lives through deep listening and prayer. Many spiritual directors are ordained clergy, while others are laity of deep faith and wisdom. As spiritual author Barbara Peacock describes it, "Spiritual Direction is a gift to the body of Christ in which one is committed to sitting with another to help that person better identify

---

[3] O'Donohue, *Anam Cara*, 25.

and experience the activity of God in his or her life."[4] Some people prefer the formal role of a spiritual director, while others appreciate a mutual relationship between Soul Friends.

I've had the privilege to find Soul Friendship in multiple relationships throughout my life. At times I sought the guidance of professional spiritual directors who listened prayerfully and pointed out the movements of God's Spirit in my life. I also have several close friends who share my interest in spirituality and personal growth. We talk about our faith, our hopes, our joys, and our grief. It hasn't always been easy to share the vulnerability of my soul, but the spiritual intimacy of these Soul Friendships has been a precious gift.

Soul Friends in Scripture and Tradition

The term Soul Friend originated in Celtic Christianity, but the concept of spiritual intimacy is as old as scripture itself. In the creation story, God saw it was not good for Adam to be alone, affirming that human beings are made to be in relationship. We see the value of companionship in the stories of Moses and Aaron, Ruth and Naomi, and David and Jonathan.[5] The leaders of God's people throughout scripture surrounded themselves with prophets and spiritual advisors who offered faithful feedback on their decisions. Even Jesus acknowledges the role of friendship, identifying his disciples as friends who share in the intimacy of knowing God.[6] When he commissions them to spread his message in nearby towns, he sends them out in pairs.[7]

In medieval Christianity, women and men known for their spiritual wisdom often served as teachers and guides to others. Many of these were priests with the authority to hear confessions and assign spiritual practices as penance. For others, however, the language of friendship best described the connection. Aelred of Rievaulx, a twelfth-century abbot, wrote a treatise titled *On Friendship* in which he identified friendship as the highest example of human love, daring even to claim, "God is friendship."[8]

---

[4] Barbara Peacock, *Soul Care in African American Practice* (Downers Grove, IL: InterVarsity Press, 2020), 64.

[5] See Genesis 2:18, Ruth 1:16–17, Exodus 4:14–16, and 1 Samuel 18:1.

[6] John 15:15

[7] Luke 10:1.

[8] Douglass Roby, "Introduction," in Aelred of Rievaulx, *Spiritual Friendship*, trans. Mary Eugenia Laker SSND (Piscataway, NJ: Gorgias Press, 2010), 17.

As Christianity spread to the British Isles, the concept of a spiritual guide merged with the pre-existing Gaelic term *anam cara*, literally "soul friend." The term originally referred to spiritual advisors who served in the courts of clan chieftains. Eventually Soul Friendship became a widespread practice, with both clergy and laity serving as spiritual guides to others.[9] An old Celtic saying attributed to Saint Brigid of Kildare says, "Anyone without a soul friend is a body without a head."[10]

Orthodox and Protestant traditions also maintained practices of spiritual guidance. Drawing from the wisdom of the early Desert Elders, Orthodox monastic traditions promoted the value of a "Spiritual Father," or *staretz* in Russian. This was usually an experienced older monk or priest who provided guidance and discernment rooted in humility and Christ-like love.[11] Protestant leaders, often wary of Catholic hierarchical structures, were careful to separate spiritual guidance from the practice of individual confession.[12] They instead emphasized the communal role of spiritual discernment and the mutuality among all believers. The common denominator across these branches of Christianity is the recognition that spiritual growth benefits from the guidance of others.

American Christianity established its own traditions of spiritual intimacy and guidance. In *Soul Care in African American Practice*, Barbara L. Peacock traces the themes of spiritual direction in African American Christianity through the lives of notable black leaders. She uses the term "soul care" to describe deep attentiveness to the spiritual well-being of another person.[13] She notes that while the language of spiritual direction is less common in African American spirituality, leaders of the black church developed practices of soul care parallel to those developed in white Christianity.[14]

Christian theologians have often reflected on human relationships as reflections of God's relational nature. Humanity was created in the image of God, and God is three persons in one, so they conclude that our reflection of God must have a communal aspect. Biblical descriptions of the church as the collective "body of Christ," with

---

[9] Kenneth Leech, *Soul Friend: Spiritual Direction in the Modern World*, rev. ed., (Harrisburg, PA: Morehouse Publishing, 2001), 45–46.

[10] Leech, *Soul Friend*, 45.

[11] Leech, *Soul Friend*, 40ff.

[12] Leech, *Soul Friend*, 81.

[13] Peacock, *Soul Care*, 4.

[14] Peacock, *Soul Care*, 156.

all its various members working in harmony, support this concept.[15] The life of faith was never intended to be a solo journey. Traditions of mentoring, guidance, and companionship develop because we grow and learn best in community. Whether it's called spiritual direction, *anam cara*, or soul care, the need for relationship and connection to maintain a healthy spirituality has always been a part of the heritage of faith.

Why Try Soul Friendship?

We are not solitary creatures. Our bodies, minds, and souls need connection with others. Many of us felt this deeply during the isolation of the COVID-19 pandemic. The rise in depression, anxiety, and substance use during the lockdowns illustrated the cost of social deprivation.[16] Our social needs are broad-ranging. Soul Friendship is just one relationship among many, but it brings an element of spiritual intimacy that can deepen our overall sense of connection.

Social connection has a real effect on our physical health. Heartbreaking studies show that infants deprived of physical contact face significant developmental issues.[17] This biological need for connection continues throughout our lives. Loneliness and isolation can increase the risk of premature death by at least 25 percent.[18] Studies have also found lack of social connection to be a risk factor for heart disease, stroke, dementia, and even common respiratory illnesses.[19] It's clear our bodies need relationships in order to thrive.

Our minds are just as dependent on our sense of connection to others. The surgeon general's advisory on loneliness highlights the way in which our brains adapted to social relationships as a survival strategy.[20] Our ancient ancestors knew there was safety in numbers.

---

[15] Romans 12:4–5; 1 Corinthians 12:12–27.

[16] Numerous studies confirm these findings. See, for example, Philip Hyland, et al., "Anxiety and Depression in the Republic of Ireland During the COVID-19 Pandemic," *Acta Psychiatrica Scandinavica* 142, no. 3 (2020): 249–256; and Elisabet Alzueta, et al., "Risk for Depression Tripled During the COVID-19 Pandemic in Emerging Adults Followed for the Last 8 Years," *Psychological Medicine* 53, no. 5 (2023): 2,156–2,163.

[17] See, for example, Ann E. Bigelow and Lela Rankin Williams, "To Have and to Hold: Effects of Physical Contact on Infants and Their Caregivers," *Infant Behavior & Development* 61 (2020): 101494, doi:10.1016/j.infbeh.2020.101494.

[18] U.S. Surgeon General, *Our Epidemic of Loneliness*, 8.

[19] U.S. Surgeon General, *Our Epidemic of Loneliness*, 8.

[20] U.S. Surgeon General, *Our Epidemic of Loneliness*, 9.

Most of us have the luxury of not facing life-or-death risks every day, but our brains are still wired to depend on others. When our social needs are not fulfilled, it can lead to increased anxiety and depression.[21] This is why social support and connectedness are protective factors for preventing suicide.[22] Connection is a necessary ingredient for our mental well-being.

The quantity of our social interactions is less significant than the quality. Most of us have experienced feeling lonely or disconnected even in a crowd of people. As an introvert, I'm particularly drawn to longer, more in-depth conversations with a few close friends. My extroverted friends tell me they, too, value the ability to connect deeply with others. There's something powerful about opening up to someone we trust. We crave the opportunity to be fully known and loved. Psychologists like Erik Erikson and Abraham Maslow recognized this need for intimacy and belonging, including it among the fundamental principles of human development.[23]

Our longing for intimacy has a spiritual root. We seek love and acceptance from something beyond ourselves. Psalm 139 is a beautiful expression of the wonder of being fully known by the Creator .[24] Human relationships are imperfect, but at their best they reflect the unconditional love of God. It can be scary to share our vulnerable thoughts and feelings with another person, but when they accept us, we experience God's grace. A Soul Friend can provide the safety we need to explore our spiritual desires and questions without fear of judgment.

An additional benefit of Soul Friendship is the insight we gain from another's perspective. We can never see ourselves fully. We need

---

[21] U.S. Surgeon General, *Our Epidemic of Loneliness*, 8.

[22] "Promote Social Connectedness and Support," Suicide Prevention Resource Center, accessed September 15, 2024, https://sprc.org/effective-prevention/a-comprehensive-approach-to-suicide-prevention/promote-social-connectedness-and-support/.

[23] Erik Erikson considered "intimacy vs. isolation" to be the primary developmental conflict (and therefore task) of young adults. Abraham Maslow placed love/belonging as the third layer of his famous pyramid of needs, just above physiological needs and safety.

[24] Psalm 139:1–6 (NRSVUE): "You have searched me, Lord, and you know me. You know when I sit and when I rise; you perceive my thoughts from afar. You discern my going out and my lying down; you are familiar with all my ways. Before a word is on my tongue, you, Lord, know it completely. You hem me in behind and before, and you lay your hand upon me. Such knowledge is too wonderful for me, too lofty for me to attain."

others to help fill in our blind spots. Having a trusted person to give us feedback and keep us accountable can be vital. In Soul Friendship, we make a commitment to hold each other responsible for our own spiritual growth. A Soul Friend can gently remind us of things we've shared in the past or provide new food for thought. They can point out when we're being too hard on ourselves, or when we're making excuses. When our anxieties pull us into selfish nearsightedness, Soul Friendship draws us back outward and helps us to see the bigger picture.

Soul Friends provide companionship, intimacy, and accountability. They remind us that our connection to God is woven together with our relationships to others. Practicing Soul Friendship adds a communal element to our spiritual development. As we share our journey with another person, we find the connection and acceptance we need to grow and thrive.

How to Practice Soul Friendship

Finding a Soul Friend can take time, but there are a variety of options. If you're interested in receiving spiritual direction from a trained professional, you can ask your faith leaders or contact local retreat centers or seminaries to ask for recommendations of spiritual directors in your area.[25] If you prefer something more mutual, consider who in your life might have a similar interest in deepening their faith. Do you have any friends with whom you already enjoy talking about spirituality? Is there anyone whom you especially trust to explore questions of faith together? Are you part of a small group or a class on spirituality that could help you connect to someone with a similar desire for Soul Friendship?

The key is finding someone you trust and feel comfortable talking to about issues of faith and personal growth. Intimacy takes time to develop, and vulnerability can feel awkward. A shared activity can sometimes create space for deeper conversation. I've enjoyed sharing a meal or going for a hike with my Soul Friends. Others I know play golf, repair cars, or work on craft projects while discussing their spiritual journeys. Choose an activity that can be done without

---

[25] There is an online directory of spiritual directors at https://www. sdicompanions.org/find-a-spiritual-director-companion/, but it is open to any provider who wishes to join and is not vetted or validated by any outside source. For choosing a director I recommend getting a personal recommendation whenever possible.

breaking the flow of conversation to ensure that the focus remains on your spiritual practice.

Be sure to clarify the boundaries and expectations of this new relationship, especially if it is a shift from how you have related to this person in the past. The following steps can help you establish a structure for your Soul Friendship.

1) Make a commitment.

It's helpful to have an initial conversation about what you and your Soul Friend each expect from the practice. How often will you meet, and for how long? What structure, if any, will shape your conversations? What boundaries will you set on topics/areas to explore? Is there an expectation of mutuality, or is one person primarily offering support and guidance to the other (as in formal spiritual direction)? How will you handle matters of confidentiality? Clarifying these things up front builds trust and prevents misunderstandings. You may even want to put your agreements in writing.

2) Meet regularly.

The length, frequency, and location of your meetings are up to you to decide, but consistency is helpful and can make it easier to stay committed. If it's easier for you to talk while engaging in a shared activity, decide what you'd like to do together. Talk with your Soul Friend about what's realistic for both of you, then stick to whatever you decide. Showing up can be the hardest part, so hold each other accountable. Remind yourselves this is a spiritual practice, not just a social conversation, and it requires intentionality.

3) Be real.

Authenticity is a necessary component of Soul Friendship. Try not to hide behind social conventions or habitual answers. Do your best to express yourself without worrying about what the other person might think. Strive to bring the fullness of your emotions and insights to the conversation.

4) Listen deeply.

Your Soul Friend may have their own questions and insights to explore, or they may share feedback on whatever you bring to the conversation. Either way, attentive listening will ensure that you're fully present and can benefit from your Soul Friend's perspective. Ask questions and explore insights together, but try to avoid giving advice or solving problems.

5) Follow up.

The benefit of meeting regularly is that it enables you to share developments over time. If a particular concern seems significant, revisit it again at the next meeting to see what has shifted. This also helps build accountability into your Soul Friendship. For example, if you discuss trying a new spiritual practice, your Soul Friend can follow up to see how it went.

Tips for Practicing Soul Friendship

If you and/or your Soul Friend are new to this practice, it can feel a little awkward at first. Below are a few topics to spark deep and soulful conversation:

- *Your spiritual journey.* How did you come to know God? What life experiences most shaped your faith? Have you had any spiritual mentors or guides?

- *Spiritual questions.* What concerns do you have about faith? What do you want to know about God? What does your spirit long for? What aspects of your spiritual life do you find unsatisfying?

- *Finding God in your life.* Where and how do you see God at work? Do you feel any sense of guidance or calling? In what parts of your life does God feel absent to you?

- *Personal prayer concerns.* What fears or worries would you like to lift up to God? What do you need help with? Is there something your Soul Friend can keep in prayer for you and/or follow up on next time you meet? Keep the focus on your own experience, rather than on a list of other people you want to pray for.

Reflection

Once you've met with your Soul Friend a few times, take a moment to reflect using the questions below. For this practice I highly recommend talking through your answers together with your Soul Friend. Reflecting together gives you both a chance to check in and share what is working or not.

- What has been the most helpful part about your Soul Friendship?
- What, if any, aspects of this practice have felt uncomfortable or difficult?
- What new insights have you gained?
- In what ways have you experienced God through this practice?
- Do you wish to continue the Soul Friend practice? If so, what adjustments would you like to make?

APPENDIX

Ways to Use This Book

Sacred Balance does not need to be read cover to cover. It's not a textbook or a homework assignment to be completed. Think of it more like a catalog you can flip through. Go into more depth on whatever topics particularly catch your eye. Some practices may draw you back again and again, while others may not feel like a good fit for you. You might return to them in various seasons of life and find they affect you differently. Feel free to hop around between chapters and try out the practices that look the most interesting at this particular time in your life.

The practices in *Sacred Balance* are intentionally flexible. Most can be done on your own or in a small group. Each can be adapted to fit your needs and context. Some readers will find this flexibility freeing, while others will prefer more clear-cut instructions. I've done my best to strike a balance between these two poles. Rest assured that while the foundations of each practice were developed centuries ago, the details continue to evolve. So try not to focus on whether you're "doing it right." Instead, focus on how well the practice is fostering your spiritual growth.

Spiritual practices are most beneficial when you can maintain them over time. The key is to find what works for you and feels sustainable. It's the same advice we often hear about physical exercise: you're more likely to keep it up if you enjoy it and it fits your lifestyle. So as you try out some of these spiritual practices, pay attention to how you feel about them and consider how well they fit your spiritual life. You can use the reflection questions at the end of each chapter to help assess what's working or not working for you.

I intend the section headings in each chapter to help you choose how deep to go. Some people like to understand the background before trying something new. Others prefer to dive into the practical steps first. Use the parts that help you, and don't worry about the rest.

What Is [the Practice]? offers a basic overview. This will give you a good sense of the practice and how it compares to other familiar practices.

Scripture and Tradition provides background on how the practice developed from a biblical and historical perspective.

Why Try [the Practice] looks at the benefits of the practice for overall well-being. This is where you'll find all the research highlighting potential mental health impacts.

How to Practice outlines concrete steps to guide you through the practice. This is the practical section where you can experience it yourself.

Tips for Practicing gives some additional suggestions for adapting the practice to suit your needs.

Reflection poses some questions to help you explore your experience more deeply. This section is designed to be used after trying the practice a few times.

If you're not sure where to start, read the brief introduction to each chapter. See if anything draws your attention or speaks to an issue you're facing. Consider your personal goals, both spiritually and in terms of mental health. Are you hoping to find more balance in a time of stress? Do you want to integrate your faith more in your day-to-day life? Identifying your goals for spiritual growth and mental well-being may guide you in exploring these practices. Take a look at this table for ideas on where you might start:

Your Goal	Practices to Try
To combat busyness	• Centering Prayer (ch. 1) • Sabbath (ch. 5) • Prayerful Savoring (ch. 8)
To increase connection	• Loving Kindness Prayer (ch. 3) • Pilgrimage (ch. 7) • Soul Friendship (ch. 9)
To integrate spirituality into your daily life	• Daily Examen (ch. 2) • Practicing the Presence of God (ch. 4) • Breath Prayer (ch. 6)
To seek guidance	• Daily Examen (ch. 2) • Soul Friendship (ch. 9)
To manage anxiety	• Loving Kindness Prayer (ch. 3) • Breath Prayer (ch. 6) • Prayerful Savoring (ch. 8)
To increase your compassion and sense of justice	• Loving Kindness Prayer (ch. 3) • Pilgrimage (ch. 7)
To deepen your awareness	• Centering Prayer (ch. 1) • Practicing the Presence of God (ch.4) • Breath Prayer (ch. 6)
To increase joy	• Daily Examen (ch. 2) • Sabbath (ch. 5) • Prayerful Savoring (ch. 8)
To re-evaluate priorities	• Daily Examen (ch. 2) • Sabbath (ch. 5) • Pilgrimage (ch. 7)

Below you'll find suggestions for using the book in different settings. I've included options for individual practice as well as various group configurations. Again, please use these guidelines only as they suit your context and needs. Feel free to be creative and let God's inspiration shape your own experience of the practices I've shared.

Self-Guided Practice

Reflect on your goals and your intention for engaging these practices. Read the introductory section of each chapter and/or use the table above to select the practices that best suit your goals. Plan on taking at least two weeks to get used to each practice. For example, if you select four practices, give yourself eight weeks.

Suggested schedule for each practice:

Week 1: Read the chapter and begin the practice.

- You can set a day to read the chapter all in one sitting or take it piecemeal throughout the week.
- Use the *How to Practice* and *Tips for Practicing* sections to get started.
- Establish a regular time and place to engage the practice.
- Keep a journal of your responses, insights, and questions.
- Remember there is no perfect way to practice. Find what works for you!

Week 2: Reflect and make adjustments.

- Use the *Reflection* section at the end of the chapter to explore your experience so far.
- Review your journal, and note any themes that are arising.
- Decide if you'd like to make any changes to the practice this week.
- Continue the practice with these adjustments, and keep reflecting.

Set aside a regular time for engaging your spiritual practices. Though this may vary from one practice to the next, establishing a set time and place will help you stay consistent. You can spend some of your designated time reading about the practice, but the goal is actually to try them out. They are called practices for a reason! Give yourself grace for days when life gets in the way. Don't give up just because you missed a day or two. As soon as you're able, return to the habit of regularly engaging in your spiritual practice.

Practice with a Soul Friend

If you already have a spiritual director or Soul Friend, you can use this book together. If you don't have someone in mind, look at the tips for finding a spiritual partner in chapter 9 under *How to Practice Soul Friendship.* For new Soul Friends, it may be helpful to discuss some of the topics listed under *Tips for Practicing Soul Friendship* in chapter 9 to establish trust and intimacy prior to engaging the other practices.

Review chapter 9 together with your Soul Friend and discuss your expectations. Select which of the other practices you intend to share, and establish a timeline of when and how often you intend to meet. I recommend trying to meet at least twice for each practice, once halfway through and again at the end before transitioning to a new practice:

First meeting (after beginning a practice):

- Review the questions in the *Reflection* section at the end of the selected practice.
- Discuss honestly any barriers that got in the way of your practice.
- Identify any changes you want to make, individually or together.
- Commit to continuing the practice for the agreed-upon timeframe.

Second meeting (at the conclusion of a practice):

- Return to the *Reflection* questions and share any new observations or insights.
- Discuss whether the practice supports your spiritual goals and if/when you might return to it in the future.
- Confirm the next practice you plan to try together.

Seven-Day Retreat

Use the following outline for a weeklong retreat (or adapt it for whatever time you have). The order of the practices shifts our focus gradually from the internal to the external. We recognize God's presence within us then follow the Spirit outward toward engagement with the world and with others. You can complete this retreat on your own, using a journal to reflect each day, or work with a spiritual director or Soul Friend who can journey with you.

Begin each day by reading a chapter. Use the notes below to help structure your practice throughout the day. End each day by prayerfully reviewing the reflection questions at the end of the chapter.

Day 1: Grounding: Breath Prayer

- Read chapter 6.
- Reflect on your breath throughout the day.
- Notice how God's support is always with you.
- Choose three to five moments during the day to stop whatever you're doing and focus solely on your breath for several minutes.
- End the day by reviewing the *Reflection* section at the end of chapter 6.

Day 2: Contemplation: Centering Prayer

- Read chapter 1.
- Dedicate several short periods throughout the day to engage in Centering Prayer.
- Ensure you have a dedicated space with minimal distractions.
- End the day by reviewing the *Reflection* section at the end of chapter 1.

Day 3: Mindfulness: Practicing the Presence of God

- Read chapter 4.
- Identify some tasks you can do in companionship with God throughout the day.
- Although this is a retreat, you still have to attend to basic tasks such as getting dressed, preparing and eating meals, and cleaning or tidying your space. Use these tasks as opportunities for practicing the Presence of God.
- End the day by reviewing the *Reflection* section at the end of chapter 4.

Day 4: Rest: Sabbath

- Read chapter 5.
- Relieve yourself of all obligations today.
- Take a nap, go for a walk, or simply rest in a comfortable place.
- Resist the urge to "accomplish" anything.
- End the day by reviewing the *Reflection* section at the end of chapter 5.

Day 5: Gratitude: Prayerful Savoring

- Read chapter 8.
- Focus on your senses throughout the day.
- Seek out pleasant experiences such as beautiful scenery, music, and food.
- Try to engage each of your five senses at some point throughout the day.
- End the day by reviewing the *Reflection* section at the end of chapter 8.

Day 6: Compassion: Loving Kindness Prayer

- Read chapter 3.
- Plan to engage the prayer at least five times during the day.
- For your first practice, start with only step one, focusing on God's love for you.
- For your second practice, repeat step 1 and add step 2, focusing on someone you care about.
- Continue adding one step each time you practice over the course of the day.
- Build up to the full prayer, including offering love to all people in the world.
- End the day by reviewing the *Reflection* section at the end of chapter 3.

Day 7: Discernment: Daily Examen

- Read chapter 2.
- Use the Daily Examen to reflect on the week, and note which practices were most helpful.
- Take note of your experiences of consolation and desolation. What might they be teaching you?
- What insights or practices from this retreat might you carry back into your daily life?
- End the day by reviewing the *Reflection* section at the end of chapter 2.

Long-Term Adult Small Group

This format assumes a committed group who all want to dive deeply into spiritual practices together. There can be a designated group leader, or participants can take turns leading. Each participant will read the chapters on their own and set aside time to practice individually. The group can meet weekly to discuss the experience and, when possible, engage in a shared practice together. Ideally, take two full weeks for each practice (eighteen weeks for the whole book).

Week 1: Discuss the chapter and practice together.

- Invite each person to read the chapter ahead of time.
- Discuss the content and share any questions, insights, or hesitations about engaging this practice.
- Offer a guided group practice when applicable (see options below).
- Encourage each person to commit to how and when they will practice on their own.

Week 2: Share experiences and reflections.

- Invite each person to share their experiences of the practice so far.
- If needed, use the questions from the *Reflection* section to guide the conversation.
- Discuss whether/how to make any adjustments in the practice.
- Encourage each person to continue the practice for another week.

Options for Shared Practices in Week 1:

Chapter 1: Offer a time of silence to engage in Centering Prayer together. The group leader can read aloud the steps from the *How to Practice Centering Prayer* section first. Use a timer so no one needs to keep an eye on the clock.

Chapter 2: Engage in a conversational version of the Daily Examen. Using the steps from the *How to Practice the Daily Examen* section, talk through the questions as a group or in pairs.

Chapter 3: Share a guided Loving Kindness Prayer together. The group leader can read the steps from *How to Practice Loving Kindness*

Prayer, or group members can take turns each reading one step of the prayer aloud. Pause after each step to allow space for the experience of compassion.

Chapter 4: Practice the Presence of God together with a shared task. Read the steps from *How to Practice the Presence of God* aloud first. Pick a simple activity that everyone in the group can engage equally. Some ideas: washing hands (bring bowls, water, soap, towels), folding something (laundry, towels, bulletins), sorting (colored beads, socks, silverware).

Chapter 5: Organize a shared Sabbath time as a group. Set clear expectations for when it should happen, how long it will last, and any limitations on types of activities (e.g., screens vs. no screens). Play games, share a meal, or just hang out and enjoy unstructured time together!

Chapter 6: Offer a guided time of Breath Prayer. Aim for three to five minutes or longer if the group is more experienced. The group leader can use the steps from *How to Practice Breath Prayer* to structure the time, or group members can read them ahead of time and practice together in silence.

Chapter 7: Take a group pilgrimage. Visit a prayer labyrinth together or identify a local volunteering opportunity. Travel together if possible, and use the time to discuss your experiences of stepping outside your comfort zones.

Chapter 8: Share a festive meal as a group. Play music, light candles, dance, and enjoy good food together. Focus on the multisensory experience and celebrate together!

Chapter 9: Divide the group into pairs (with sensitivity to levels of trust). Groups of three are fine if you have an odd number of participants. Use the discussion prompts under *Tips for Practicing Soul Friendship* to engage in spiritual reflection together. Encourage the Soul Friends to meet again on their own, or use Week 2 to pair off again and follow up on the practice.

Short-Term Adult Education Class

This is a lighter, more accessible group format. It's great for workshops, classes with inconsistent attendance, or groups with lower commitment level. It requires a designated group leader (or two) who can read the material in depth and present it in an engaging way. Encourage group members to read the chapters and try out the practices, but there is no expectation that they must do so. Plan one week for each practice selected. The sample below is a suggestion for a four-week series.

Week 1: Daily Examen

- Invite group members to read chapter 2 ahead of time.
- Group leader presents highlights from the chapter:
  - What is discernment?
  - How do we look for God in our lives?
  - What do consolation and desolation look like?
- Offer a guided Daily Examen practice using the steps from *How to Practice the Daily Examen*.
- Invite group discussion/reflection on the experience.

Week 2: Loving Kindness Prayer

- Invite group members to read chapter 3 ahead of time.
- Group leader presents highlights from the chapter:
  - Why should we love our enemies?
  - What is *agape* love?
  - Our love is grounded in God's love for us.
- Offer a guided Loving Kindness Prayer using the steps from *How to Practice Loving Kindness Prayer*.
- Invite group discussion/reflection on the experience.

Week 3: Breath Prayer

- Invite group members to read chapter 6 ahead of time.
- Group leader presents highlights from the chapter:
  - What is grounding?
  - Breath is linked to Spirit in the Bible.
  - Breath is a tool we always carry with us.
- Offer a guided Breath Prayer using the steps from *How to Practice Breath Prayer*.
- Invite group discussion/reflection on the experience.

Week 4: Prayerful Savoring

- Invite group members to read chapter 8 ahead of time.
- Group leader presents highlights from the chapter:
- What is savoring?
- What is the "negativity bias"?
- How do our senses help us connect to God?
- Offer a sensory experience such as a shared meal, listening to music, or using essential oils. Encourage group members to focus on their senses as a source of gratitude.
- Invite group discussion/reflection on the experience.

Youth

Young people need to integrate faith and daily life just as much as adults do.[1] The youth mental health crisis has become a fact of life. The good news is teenagers increasingly have experience talking about mental health issues. We have a great opportunity to bring faith into these conversations, and the practices in this book offer a concrete starting place. The material can be adapted for use in a youth group or Sunday school context. The key will be knowing your particular youth—their interests, their struggles, and what they might be willing to try. Youth leaders can read the chapters and use them as a springboard for shaping lessons and activities. I've offered some general tips and suggestions for each practice below. Use your own creativity and judgment to tailor the practices to your particular needs.

General Tips:[2]

- Use the scripture verse(s) at the top of the chapter and the discussion questions under *Reflection* to help frame each practice.

---

[1] For more on engaging youth in contemplative spiritual practices, check out Mark Yaconelli's *Contemplative Youth Ministry: Practicing the Presence of Jesus* (Grand Rapids, MI: Zondervan, 2006).

[2] Credit for these tips and many of the specific practice suggestions goes to my friend and colleague Ellen White. Her wisdom and heart for the experiences of young people is an inspiration.

- Break down the basic concept of the practice and relate it to teens' experiences.
- Offer a variety of engagement options to accommodate different learning styles.

Specific Practices:

Contemplation: Centering Prayer (Ch. 1)

- Talk about stillness. Where and how do they experience it? Is it comfortable? Uncomfortable?
- Highlight the difference between contemplation/stillness and "mindless" screen time. Discuss what thoughts and feelings come up when sitting without distractions.
- Invite them to imagine someone they can sit with comfortably in silence. What might it be like to sit with God in that way?
- Offer a short, guided Centering Prayer practice.

Discernment: Daily Examen (Ch. 2)

- Focus on choices: What choices are they making in their lives? What factors influence their choices? Does faith play a role? If so, how?
- Share some definitions of the word "discernment" and ask for real-life examples.
- Ask if/how they see God in their lives. Talk about ways we can recognize God.
- Share "highs and lows" from the week, and discuss what they reveal about God.

Compassion: Loving Kindness Prayer (Ch. 3)

- Share about different types of love (romantic/friendship/*agape*, etc.). Ask for examples of each.
- Talk about "enemies" and what it means to love them. Emphasize that love doesn't mean letting yourself be victimized.
- Invite them to create artwork (visual art, music, poetry, etc.) expressing their sense of God's love.
- Offer a guided practice of the Loving Kindness Prayer.

Mindfulness: Practicing the Presence of God (Ch. 4)

- Talk about doing chores. Do they feel different when doing them with a friend?
- Discuss being on "autopilot" vs. fully aware. Invite them to act out the difference in various scenarios.
- Describe the example of washing each dish like it's the baby Jesus (found under *Tips for Practicing the Presence of God*).
- Engage them in a simple project like washing dishes or folding paper. Invite them to notice God's presence during the task.

Rest: Sabbath (Ch. 5)

- Discuss the Sabbath commandment: What's the point of it? Why does God want us to rest?
- Ask them to list things in their life from which they might need rest (e.g., school, social events, technology, etc.).
- Use the image of a heavy backpack: What are they carrying around? What can be taken out to lighten the load?

Breath Prayer (Ch. 6)

- Share the biblical imagery of God as wind/breath.
- Invite them to pause and notice their breath for one to two minutes then to share their observations.
- Offer a guided breath prayer, or use this video created by the Center for Action and Contemplation: https://www.youtube.com/watch?v=vOoeGnN8YTc.

Pilgrimage (Ch. 7)

- Take the group on a trip to visit a church of a different cultural tradition, or engage in a service project together.
- Print out finger labyrinths and talk about using them as a tool for prayer, or find a labyrinth in your area to walk/roll.
- Discuss the value of being uncomfortable and ask for examples.
- Take a prayer walk/roll around the neighborhood, and invite the youth to reflect on the needs of the community.

Prayerful Savoring (Ch. 8)

- Invite the youth to bring in their favorite music, art, or foods to share with each other. Invite them to talk about what they appreciate about it.
- Offer a guided mindful tasting practice such as this one: https://www.va.gov/WHOLEHEALTHLIBRARY/docs/Script-Mindful-Eating.pdf.
- Talk about gratitude, and ask the youth to notice how it feels when they think about things they enjoy.

Soul Friends (Ch. 9)

- Discuss what makes for good friendship, then ask what would be different if a spiritual element was added.
- Talk about listening, and practice a one-minute listening exercise in pairs.
- Take care "assigning" Soul Friend partners to ensure every person's trust and safety.
- Adult mentors could act as Soul Friends to youth as long as all involved know and follow your community's child protection guidelines to ensure each person's safety.

Younger Children

Several of the practices in this book are very concrete, making them a great option to use with elementary age children. You can tell a Bible story and use the practice to help children engage in a multi-sensory way. These spiritual practices can help children develop a toolbox of ways to connect with God. The following are the practices I recommend for this age group, with some suggestions for how you might present them:

Breath Prayer (Ch. 6)

- Tell the creation story, focusing on God as the wind/spirit moving across the water and God breathing life into Adam and Eve.
- Talk about how we can't see air, but it's all around us, just like God.
- Have each child place their hands on their belly and feel it move as they breathe in and out.
- Offer a simple prayer phrase to pair with breathing, such as "Jesus loves me" (*inhale*) "this I know" (*exhale*).

Prayerful Savoring (Ch. 8)

- Read Psalm 136:1–9.
- Talk about gratitude, and invite children to share what they're thankful for.
- Talk about the five senses and how they help us appreciate what God gives us.
- Share ideas for using each of the five senses to express faith (e.g., give a hug, listen to a favorite hymn, look at Bible story pictures, taste communion bread).
- Share a snack together, and ask children to notice the taste and texture of the food. Offer a simple prayer of *"Thank you God for..."* for each thing they notice.

Loving Kindness Prayer (Ch. 4)

- Tell the story of the good Samaritan.
- What does it feel like to be loved? How do you know when someone loves you?
- Describe God's love for us and how it overflows as we share love with others.
- Talk about kindness, and share examples of showing kindness to someone.
- Use a simple fill-in-the-blank version of the Loving Kindness Prayer. "God loves me. / God loves ... [*friend/family member*] / God loves ...[*someone you don't know very well*] / God loves... [*someone you don't always like*] / God loves everyone."

Sabbath (Ch. 5)

- Read the Sabbath commandment from Exodus 20:9–10.
- Ask: Why does God want us to rest?
- Invite children to list things from which they need to take breaks (e.g., school, homework, chores, etc.).
- Talk about how our bodies need rest. Ask how they feel when they're tired vs. well-rested.
- Ask children to share their favorite things to do when taking a break.

ACKNOWLEDGEMENTS

As I wrote in chapter 9, the life of faith is not a solitary journey. Neither is writing a book! *Sacred Balance* would not be here without the contributions of many amazing souls. I built on the foundation of generations of faithful people who shared their spiritual wisdom. I'm also blessed by the fellowship of particular friends, family, and colleagues who helped make this book a reality.

First of all, I want to thank my mother, Evelyn Diephouse, who nurtured my love of theology and mystical wisdom. She was my first spiritual director and my greatest cheerleader. When *Sacred Balance* was just an idea, she saw its potential and encouraged me to seek publication. Thank you, Mom, for convincing me I could bless others with my passion and insight.

I am infinitely grateful to my husband, Philip McMillan, for supporting me in all things, including this project. He listened to my rambling ideas and edited my rambling sentences. He did more than his share of parenting and housework to give me time to write. Thank you, Phil, for being my steady rock through it all.

Several good friends and colleagues read my early drafts and shared their wisdom. Ali Van Kuiken was my constant conversation partner and confidant. Diane Kenaston and Ben Gosden kept me accountable to my deadlines and honed my writing skills. Rebekah Anderson and Christina Keddie reviewed my final manuscript with precision and grace.

Many others shaped my understanding of faith and mental health throughout my career. My supervisors Dwight Sweezy and MaryJane Inman recognized and nurtured my calling to chaplaincy. Kerri Erbig was both a mentor and friend along the way. I'm also grateful to all the patients who shared their stories with me and participated in my groups. Their faith and resilience remain an inspiration.

I'd like to thank the community of Pennington Presbyterian Church, particularly the Mental Health Task Force and small group who planted the seeds of *Sacred Balance* back in 2020. Thanks to Ellen White for sharing her expertise with all things youth to ensure that this book can benefit people of all ages.

Finally, I want to thank the wonderful people of Chalice Press and Young Clergy Women International. Brad Lyons believed in this project and made it real with his enthusiasm. Ulrike Guthrie was a thoughtful and collaborative editor. Diane Kenaston and Courtney Smith Westerlund guided me through submission, publication, and publicity with efficient care. And though I no longer qualify as "young," the YCWI community has been a siblinghood of support for many years.